SECRET
MONTREAL
AN UNUSUAL GUIDE

Philippe Renault

Jonglez

We have taken great pleasure in drawing up
Secret Montreal and hope that through its guidance
you will, like us, continue to discover unusual,
hidden or little-known aspects of the city.
Descriptions of certain places are accompanied
by thematic sections highlighting historical details
or anecdotes as an aid to understanding the city in
all its complexity.
Secret Montreal also draws attention
to the multitude of details found in places
that we may pass every day without noticing.
These are an invitation to look more closely
at the urban landscape and, more generally,
a means of seeing our own city with the curiosity
and attention that we often display while travelling
elsewhere …

Comments on this guidebook and its contents, as well
as information on places we may not have mentioned,
are more than welcome and will enrich future
editions.

Don't hesitate to contact us:
• Éditions Jonglez, 17, boulevard du Roi,
   78000 Versailles, France
• E-mail: info@jonglezpublishing.com

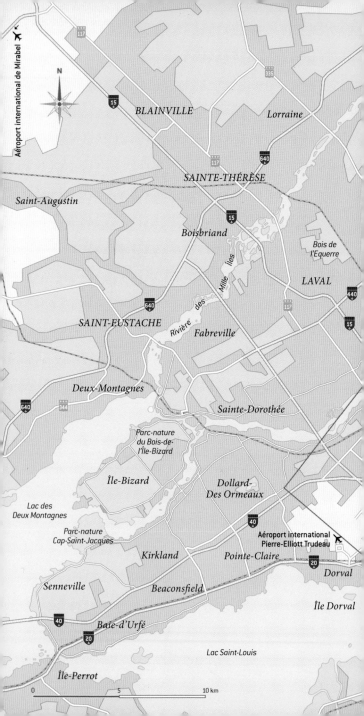

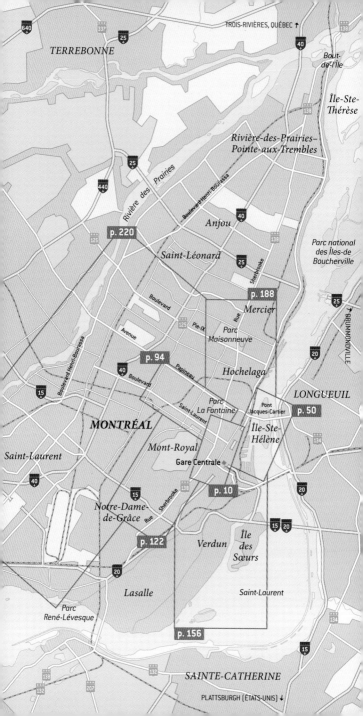

CONTENTS

SAINT-LAURENT, SAINT-DENIS, PLATEAU

MONT-ROYAL, OUTREMONT, WESTMOUNT, NDG

CONTENTS

WEST CENTRAL AND SOUTH-WEST

EAST CENTRAL AND EAST MONTREAL

ROSEMONT, MONTREAL NORTH AND THE WEST OF THE ISLAND

INDEX

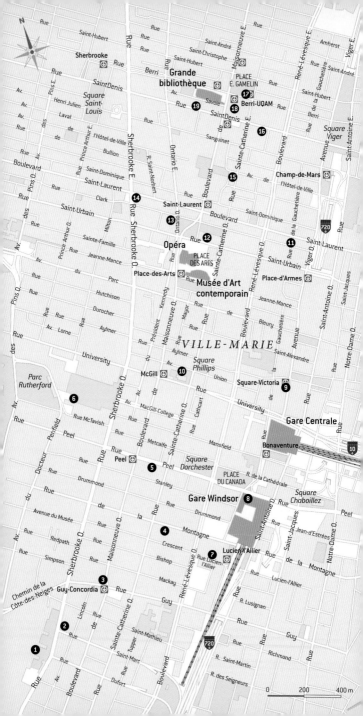

VILLE-MARIE, DOWNTOWN

GRAND SÉMINAIRE ❶

2065, rue Sherbrooke Ouest
• Free guided tours (voluntary donations suggested) lasting around 1½ hours, in June, July and August, from Tuesday to Saturday at 1 pm and 3 pm
• Tel: 514 935 7775

> *A historic oasis in the city centre*

Entering the Grand Séminaire de Montréal (Great Seminary) is like opening a history book. The first Sulpician missionaries settled here in 1676 with the primary goal of evangelizing American Indians. Ten years later, the site was fortified with towers and curtain walls; dwellings, a chapel and agricultural buildings were added. When the evangelizing mission was moved to Sault-au-Récollet in 1692, the Messieurs de Saint-Sulpice Fort, or Fort de la Montagne (Mountain Fort), became a place of peace and meditation for the priests.

The Grand Séminaire was founded in 1840 at the request of Monsignor Bourget, Bishop of Montreal, and it became the seat of the Faculty of Theology in 1878. In 1967, the faculty moved to the University of Montreal campus, on the other side of the mountain. Today, classes are still given at the Grand Séminaire, under the auspices of the Pontifical Lateran University in Rome.

The architectural complex has been extended several times since it was established in the 19th century. Of the original fort, only two stone towers built by the Sulpician François Vachon de Belmont remain. They feature among the city's oldest constructions and have been listed as a historic monument. Marguerite Bourgeoys, the first teacher in Ville-Marie (Montreal), taught in one of these towers. Next, the tour leads to the estate's gardens and its large pool, which is exceptional not only for its size but also its history. It is the third pool built at the mountain estate, probably between 1731 and 1747 (the first two pools are no longer there); the pool was restored in 1801 and again in 1990. Framed by hundred-year-old trees, this stretch of water is 158 metres long and 8 metres wide and is fed by a drainage pool and an old spring that flows from the slopes of Mont-Royal (Mount Royal). The tour continues inside, where you'll discover the seminary's remarkable chapel. Built in 1864 to designs by architect John Ostell, it was extended in 1903 and 1907 and decorated in the Beaux-Arts style that was so popular at the time.

Thanks to an anonymous donor, a brand new organ was installed

to celebrate the 150th anniversary of the diocese of Montreal, in 1990. Concerts are given in the chapel during the Couleurs de l'Orgue Français (French Organ) festival held annually in October.

MONTREAL MASONIC MEMORIAL TEMPLE ❷

2295, rue Saint-Marc and 1850, rue Sherbrooke Ouest
• Tel: 514 933 6739
• Métro: Guy-Concordia
• Guided tours by appointment only by calling 514 933 6432, during the
annual Open Day in spring, or during special events such as concerts

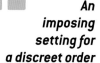

**An
imposing
setting for
a discreet order**

The imposing Masonic temple at 1850, rue Sherbrooke Ouest is the primary meeting site for Montreal's Freemasons.

Its neoclassical, Beaux-Arts façade serves as a frame for a collection of Masonic symbols.

The temple consists of three levels embodying the three stages of Masonic life: a very high base, which includes the entrance, rises to nearly half the building's height; a floor decorated by four large columns and two pilasters; and, dominating the façade, a pediment below which are inscribed the words "MASONIC MEMORIAL TEMPLE", a reminder that the structure was built in 1928–29 in homage to the members of the order killed in the First World War.

The monumental bronze entrance door is flanked by two octagonal columns topped by winged horses and two spheres, one celestial and the other terrestrial. Also on the façade is a frieze containing the motto *Fides, Caritas, Veritas, Libertas, Spes* (Faith, Charity, Truth, Liberty, Hope) and the Freemason symbols of the square and compasses. Inside, you'll find remarkable woodwork and Victorian furniture decorating Lodge Room One.

The history of the Freemasons of Canada dates

back to the beginning of colonization. Soon after having conquered Quebec in 1759, the officers of General James Wolfe founded a Provincial Grand Lodge, thus establishing a Masonic power in the territory won by Great Britain. Before, the francophone Freemasons would have met in New France in the Lodge of the Restored Freemasons, which was probably founded after 1743. The headquarters of the Provincial Grand Lodge were transferred from Quebec to Montreal in 1788 by Sir John Johnson, the Grand Master at the time, who lived in Montreal.

Despite this distant Masonic presence, it wasn't until the 19th century, in 1825, that the first true temple was established in the city, on the site now occupied by Marché Bonsecours. Destroyed by fire in 1833, the temple was moved from site to site before finally leaving rue Dorchester for its new home at the corner of rue Sherbrooke and rue Saint-Marc.

On June 22, 1929, 2,000 members of the fraternity marched from the old temple to the new site to lay the building's first stone according to Masonic rites.

Surprisingly, the Masonic Temple faces the Grand Séminaire de Montréal, and thus stands opposite an entity with which it has been in conflict in the past, notably during most of the 19th century. At the time, Monsignor Bourget, Bishop of Montreal, particularly denounced this Freemasonry whose members, he believed, were stirring up "dark plots" against religion and the state.

NORMAN
BETHUNE

STATUE OF NORMAN BETHUNE ❸

Place Norman-Bethune
• Métro: Guy-Concordia

> *In honour of a hero more Chinese than Canadian*

In the small triangular island at the intersection of rue Guy and boulevard de Maisonneuve stands the statue of a hero that the majority of Canadians have never heard of. This doctor, humanist and visionary was called Norman Bethune and although he has remained an obscure figure in America, he has become a hero in China.

Born north of Toronto in Gravenhurst, Ontario, Bethune chose to follow a career in medicine. At the outbreak of the First World War, he joined the Field Ambulance as a stretcher-bearer in 1915, serving on the Belgium battlefields where he was injured by a mortar shell. Back in Canada, he finished his medical studies and enrolled in the Royal Marines as a surgeon. Between the world wars, he lived in Scotland, where he married, then in the United States, where he became infected with tuberculosis. It was during a stay in a New York sanatorium that he became aware of the inadequate treatment then given to the numerous patients. Later settled in Montreal where he worked at the Royal Victoria Hospital and the Sacré-Coeur Hospital, he dedicated eight years of his life to the study of this terrible disease. During this period, from 1928 to 1936, he invented or modified no less than twelve surgical instruments (some of which are still in use today) and published a great number of innovative articles on thoracic surgery.

Convinced of the relevance of social medicine, he admired the Soviet health system and didn't hesitate to join the Communist Party in 1935 in order to "make this world a better place". Unfortunately, his proposals for a universal health service received little support from the political elite at the time. Disappointed, Norman Bethune went elsewhere to try to improve the lives of the less fortunate. First, he went to Spain, which was on the verge of civil war, and set up mobile blood transfusion units. In rather pragmatic fashion, he gave each blood donor a bottle of wine! Then, returning for a while to Montreal, he set up a Canadian-American mobile unit that subsequently joined the army of Mao Zedong in China in 1938, when the country was at war with the Japanese invaders. In indescribable conditions and travelling by mule through the mountains, he followed the troops and performed operations, thus saving several thousand lives all while teaching the rudiments of medicine to hundreds of followers. In his self-sacrificing way, he cut his finger while operating on a soldier with his bare hands, later succumbing to blood poisoning on November 12, 1939. Nearly all Chinese citizens know about Bethune, whose story is taught in schools. So, when Montreal decided to name a square after him in the 1970s, the People's Republic of China gave the city a statue of the surgeon. The square, long known by Montreal residents as "pigeon square" due to the large number of birds that flock here for some unknown reason, was restored in 2008 to celebrate the 70th anniversary of Norman Bethune's departure for China – a rather late tribute to a hero of the Long March.

MÉDIATHÈQUE LITTÉRAIRE GAËTAN DOSTIE ❹

1214, rue de la Montagne
• Métro: Peel or Lucien-L'Allier
• Open Tuesday to Thursday, 1 pm to 5 pm or by appointment
• Admission $10
• Tel: 514 861 0880 • info@mlgd.ca

The poetic memory of Quebec

I n this neighbourhood devoted to hockey fans – Centre Bell is just nearby – and the evening barflies of nearby rue Crescent, setting up a multimedia museum dedicated to Quebecker poetry and literature in a beautiful 1845 house with blue shutters was original, to say the least. Its creator, the poet, publisher, video director, producer and collector Gaëtan Dostie, is just as original.

"It's the museum of a missionary of poetry," declared Chloé Sainte-Marie, singer and girlfriend of the late filmmaker Gilles Carle. A real enthusiast since the age of 9 when he began collecting literary materials from Quebec, Gaëtan Dostie has spent over five decades amassing documents from francophone America. More than 400 rare works by Nelligan, Miron, Borduas and other Quebecker artists are exhibited on the walls of the library's ten rooms and numerous corridors. The poem "Speak White" by Michèle Lalonde, the original copy No. 15 of the *Refus Global* manifesto that once belonged to Claude Gauvreau, and the very first anthology of the poetry of Quebec

published in 1830 figure among the gems housed here. The museum also possesses more than 500 hours of video interviews with Quebecker writers.

Nevertheless, the library's daily star turn is still its owner: it's impossible to resist the erudition and passion of Gaëtan Dostie, who generally guides visitors through this temple of Quebecker literature – a visit that is both instructive and original.

SONG AND POETRY EVENINGS IN THE GRAND SALON
Eight times a year, song and poetry evenings are held in the Grand Salon, with prestigious guests such as Jim Corcoran, Richard Séguin, Luc de la Rochellière, Michel Rivard, and even Jean-Paul Daoust and the urban rock poet Lucien Francoeur.

MARTLET HOUSE

⑤

McGill University Alumni Association
1430, rue Peel
• Métro: Peel

A Scottish manor for a Canadian whisky producer

The surprising building of limestone blocks at 1430, rue Peel is still called "the castle", a nickname it earned when it housed the headquarters of the large Canadian distillers Seagram.

Today it is home to the McGill University Alumni Association, and was officially renamed Martlet House (see below) in 2004.

Built in 1928, "the castle" is the work of architect David Jerome Spence. At the time, the Distillers Corporation Limited, founded in Montreal by Samuel Bronfman, had just acquired the Seagram distillery in Ontario. Business was booming thanks to Prohibition, enforced across the border in the United States.

The new company headquarters needed to reflect its new growth. Samuel Bronfman chose the site of the headquarters himself, right in the centre of the rich Golden Square Mile district. The building's façade is inspired by that of a 16th-century Scottish baronial castle, as a way of proving the excellent quality of the company's whisky, even though it is produced in Canada. Note

the numerous Scottish references, and notably the medallion depicting the great 18th-century poet Robert Burns (also known as Rabbie or Robbie). This "bard of Ayrshire" also has his own statue nearby in Dorchester square.

McGill University has owned the building since 2002, thanks to a donation from the Vivendi Universal Company who acquired the building when it merged with Seagram. The building on rue Peel was one of Seagram's two main offices; the other is in New York.

Martlet is the English heraldic name of a bird from the swift family. Three of these birds appear on the coat of arms of the famous McGill University, an English-language institution. It was directly inspired by the coat of arms of its founder, James McGill.

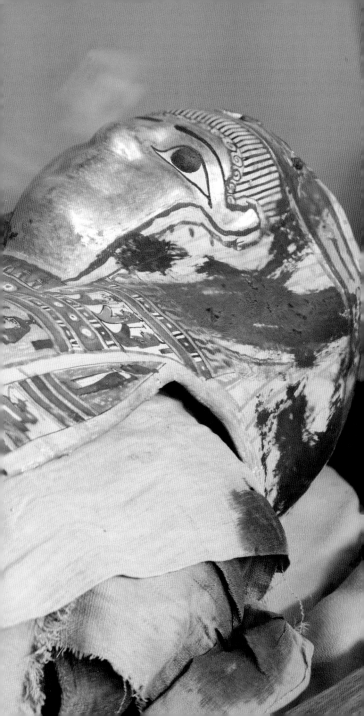

MUSÉE REDPATH'S MUMMIES

859, rue Sherbrooke Ouest on McGill University campus
• Métro: McGill, University exit
• Open Monday to Friday, 9 am to 5 pm and Sunday, 1 pm to 5 pm, with discovery workshops; closed Saturdays and public holidays
• Tel: 514 398 4092 and 514 398 4086, ext. 00549
• Admission free. Suggested donations for the general public: students and children $2, adults $5

T he Redpath Museum is exactly the sort of special place we love to discover: a haven of culture that has that indescribable scent of beeswax and ancient objects.

The old ladies of the university

Linked to the prestigious McGill University's Faculty of Science, it is the oldest natural history museum in Canada. Nearly 3 million artefacts covering the fields of palaeontology, geology, zoology, ethnology and mineralogy fill the three floors of the museum.

The building is probably one of the most remarkable on the campus. The museum was built thanks to a donation from Peter Redpath, an industrialist who made his fortune in the sugar business, and is the work of architects Hutchison and Steele – a remarkable, although late, example of North American Greek Revival architecture.

Inaugurated in 1882 to house the collection of Sir William Dawson, a great naturalist and principal of the university at the time, the museum was originally reserved solely for students and researchers. It wasn't opened to the general public until 1952.

The most spectacular pieces are the famous dinosaur skeletons displayed at

the centre of the Dawson gallery, which was restored in 2003. A *Gorgosaurus libratus* bares its sharp teeth to visitors as they enter. Other more discreet stars of the collection are displayed on the top floor.

Of the three mummies brought back from Egypt in 1859 by businessman and future Montreal mayor James Ferrier, only two are on display; the third is too fragile. The oldest mummy is around 3,500 years old. A hieroglyph-covered coffin, various mummified animals, a selection of pottery and a replica of the Rosetta Stone, which served to decipher Egyptian hieroglyphs, complete this remarkable collection of Egyptian antiquities, unfortunately little known.

THE "GUARANTEED PURE MILK" BOTTLE

1025, rue Lucien-L'Allier
• Also visible from place du Centenaire of Centre Bell among the statues of great hockey players
• Métro: Lucien-L'Allier

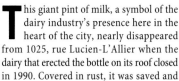

The giant pint of milk

This giant pint of milk, a symbol of the dairy industry's presence here in the heart of the city, nearly disappeared from 1025, rue Lucien-L'Allier when the dairy that erected the bottle on its roof closed in 1990. Covered in rust, it was saved and restored in 2009 by Héritage Montréal, an association created to promote and protect the city's architectural, historic, natural and cultural landmarks.

In the early 19th century, Montreal residents still bought their milk from milkmen who delivered their bottles by cart. It wasn't until 1926, after several tragic cases of food poisoning, that a law was passed requiring dairies to pasteurize their milk. Founded in 1900, "Guaranteed Pure Milk" was the first dairy plant in Quebec. In 1930, at the construction of his new dairy at 1025 Aqueduct (now rue Lucien-L'Allier), owner George Hogg decided to pull a publicity stunt, in part to restore confidence in the dairy products affected by the crisis of previous years. Rather than building an ordinary water tank for the fire protection system, he had his workers build an enormous bottle of milk that could be seen all round the district. An icon was born.

Standing nearly 10 metres tall, the riveted steel bottle weighs 6 tonnes, including its base, and can hold up to 250,000 litres of water.

The Guaranteed Pure Milk and Co dairy, built in 1930, is a beautiful example of Art Deco industrial architecture. It is the work of architects Hutchison, Wood and Miller, who are also behind other remarkable buildings in the city, such as the Shaughnessy Duluth and Canadian Express buildings in Old Montreal, Victoria Hall in Westmount, the Birks jewellery store on place Phillips and the McCord Museum. Since it closed the building has become a popular film location thanks to its period decor, some of which has been preserved in its original state, including George Hogg's former office. In the future, the building will be an integral part of the project led by the promoters of E-Commerce Place, who will determine the fate of this former dairy and its famous pint of milk.

LOBBY OF WINDSOR STATION

1160, avenue des Canadiens-de-Montréal (formerly rue de la Gauchetière)
• Métro: Bonaventure or Lucien-L'Allier
• Open to the public on weekdays 6:15 am to 9:20 pm, Saturday 8:15 am to 11 pm, and Sunday 1 pm to 9 pm

The masterpiece of a heritage station

Windsor Station intrigues visitors not only by its resemblance to a medieval castle, but also by the fact that no train has stopped here since 1991.

When the Canadian Pacific Railway undertook the construction of a new train station and company headquarters in 1887, business was booming. It had just finished the western railroad that unified the country from coast to coast and launched a vast programme to build hotels and stations all along the network. The new headquarters of this influential rail company needed to reflect its power and wealth. This delicate task was entrusted to American architect Bruce Price (the designer of Quebec's Château Frontenac). He submitted four versions of his project before finally meeting the expectations of William Van Horne, the Canadian Pacific chairman.

This structure, inspired by Roman and medieval architecture, was built in the Richardson style popular in North America at the time and which is characterized by the use of solid stone and semi-circular arches, thus giving the façade its dramatic appearance. Montreal's main station was extended in 1900 and in 1909, and an impressive tower was added in 1914. At this time, the vast and modern lobby, a long cathedral of glass and metal, was also built.

Countless immigrants heading for Ontario or the Canadian prairies, followed a few years later by thousands of soldiers from the two world wars, passed through this lobby, making it a place of remembrance. Inaugurated in 1922, the *Angel of Victory* monument by Montreal sculptor Cœur-de-Lion McCarthy still graces the lobby. It is dedicated to the memory of Canadian Pacific employees killed in action.

In the 1960s, Windsor Station declined. The last intercity train left the station in 1981 and, ten years later, the last suburban train followed. Finally, in 1996, the company headquarters were transferred to Calgary. Listed as a Canadian historic landmark in 1975, as a heritage train station in 1990, and a historic landmark of Quebec in 2009, Windsor Station once risked being demolished to make way for office buildings. Having lost its rails when the nearby Centre Bell was built, it is now a phantom station, hence its unique charm. Today, the building is nothing more than the entrance to the new Lucien-L'Allier suburban and métro stations. Yet, from time to time, it also serves as the venue for special events and evening galas.

SQUARE-VICTORIA MÉTRO ENTRANCE

601, rue Saint-Antoine Ouest

Just like Paris!

I n 1966, the RATP (the Paris public transport company) loaned the brand new Montreal métro system one of Hector Guimard's famous station entrances dating from the early days of the Parisian network. According to a letter from the period, the duration of the loan "should last until time immemorial".

The Art Nouveau entrance was installed at Victoria station in 1967 to commemorate the alliance between France and Quebec during the métro's construction. Unfortunately, due to different construction codes, the Montreal entrance was larger than those in France, so the most characteristic element – the part above the stairs with a sign reading "Métropolitain" – couldn't be installed. They made do with a truncated version. Later, the work was damaged and one of the escutcheons attached to its base was even stolen.

It clearly needed a little freshening up. So, in 2001 to 2002, the STM (Société de Transport de Montréal) and RATP experts once again collaborated to undertake meticulous renovations. They took advantage of the opportunity to scale down the entrance so they could add the original "Métropolitain" sign and replace the missing elements. The interior walls of the staircase were even covered with the same white bevelled tiles used in the Paris métro. During the restoration, they discovered that Montreal's "Guimard" still had its original glass globes, the last ones surviving in the world, as Paris had already replaced theirs with plastic ones for security reasons. As a sign of gratitude, one of the globes was given to the RATP and the other to the Montreal Museum of Fine Arts.

THE ONLY ORIGINAL

In the past few years, several other Guimard-style entrances have been offered to the métro systems of Lisbon, Mexico City, Chicago and, most recently, Moscow, but these are only copies. Only the Montreal métro can boast of owning an original.

RAOUL WALLENBERG
1912 - ?

In wartime Budapest in 1944, this Christian Swedish diplomat, through his
humanity, great courage and compassion, rescued tens of thousands of
Hungarian Jews and others from certain death in the Holocaust.
War is an example of the capacity of one person's actions to overcome evil.

Under the name of the brutal Nazi occupiers and their cohorts, Wallenberg
established safe houses under the Swedish Flag and issued many thousands of
Swedish "safe passes," thus affording shelter, food, and protection to those who
would have otherwise surely perished.

Arrested and imprisoned by the Soviet authorities in January 1945,
he was never released and his fate remains unknown.
He was made an Honourary Citizen of Canada in 1985.

"Whoever saves one life, it is as if they have saved the entire world." — Talmud

En 1944 à Budapest pendant la guerre, ce diplomate suédois
chrétien, a sauvé des centaines de milliers de Juifs hongrois et
autres d'une extermination certaine durant l'Holocauste et
démontre le seul courage et à sa compassion. Son action à une
personne peut vaincre le mal.

Face à la brutalité des occupants nazis et de leurs com-
plices, Wallenberg a mis en place des résidences sous protection de la Suède et a émis des milliers de laissez-passer
suédois, procurant ainsi abri, nourriture et protection à
des milliers de gens qui autrement auraient certainement péri.

Arrêté et emprisonné par les autorités soviétiques
en janvier 1945, il ne fut jamais relâché et son sort
demeure inconnu.
Il fut fait Citoyen Honoraire du Canada en 1985.

PLACE RAOUL WALLENBERG

Behind Christ Church Anglican Cathedral between avenue Union and rue University
• Métro: McGill

> *In memory of the "Angel of Budapest"*

It's a pretty little shaded square filled with flowers and greenery, right behind Christ Church Cathedral and the bustle of rue Sainte-Catherine. Since few know of it, tourists don't often venture here. Instead, you'll generally find the employees of the numerous nearby offices. This is where Montreal decided to pay homage to someone who made his mark on the history of humanity: Raoul Wallenberg, the Angel of Budapest.

His story is an extraordinary one. Born near Stockholm in 1912 to a rich family, he studied architecture in the United States before becoming a businessman with a love for travel. In 1944, during the Second World War, he was chosen by the American War Refugee Board to organize the rescue programme for the Jews of Budapest.

From July 1944 to January 1945, Raoul Wallenberg helped tens of thousands of Hungarian Jews escape from Nazi-occupied Budapest. As the head secretary of the Swedish legation in Budapest, he facilitated the delivery of "passports" (in fact, a simple piece of paper depicting three crowns, the symbol of Sweden) to Jews, who thus took on the status of foreign citizens and were housed in buildings acquired by Sweden. Ingenious and methodical, Raoul Wallenberg was an intense negotiator who saved as many as 100,000 people, according to certain estimations, from the hands of the Nazis. He disappeared in circumstances that remain a mystery after being captured by the Soviets and probably accused of espionage. Place Raoul Wallenberg is a not only a perfect spot to take a break, but an inspiration and reminder of contemporary history.

The Angel of Budapest became one of the "Righteous Among The Nations" once this honour was created in 1963 by the Yad Vashem Memorial in Israel for non-Jews who risked their own lives to help Jews during the Holocaust.

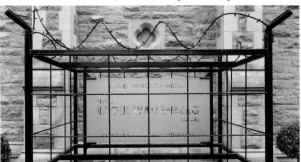

LE ROI SINGE DE CHINATOWN SCULPTURE ⓫

Rue Saint-Urbain at the corner of rue de La Gauchetière
• Métro: Place-d'Armes

A Chinese legend

At the corner of rue Saint-Urbain and rue de La Gauchetière, the street sculpture *Le Roi Singe de Chinatown* is composed of seven 5 metre high concrete panels.

The work of artist Pang Tin Neon, it illustrates the story of the Monkey King who, according to Chinese legend, became the king of the animals thanks to his shrewd nature.

At the bottom of the composition, the king on horseback is followed by his valet, who carries the luggage. In the centre, a pig on a cloud wears farmer's clothes and holds a rake. Above, on another cloud, a monkey wearing a martial arts uniform holds a staff while squatting like a pelican. In the upper left-hand corner, a palace rides on yet another cloud.

Across rue de La Gauchetière, still on rue Saint-Urbain, a bas-relief by Andrew Lui depicts musicians marching up to heaven. These two works were erected in 1984 and 1986 at the entrance to Montreal's Chinatown,

delineated by rue Viger, rue Saint-Urbain, boulevard René-Lévesque and boulevard Saint-Laurent.

Although many Chinese arrived in Canada in the mid-19th century to work on the railroad in the West, it wasn't until 1902 that this small neighbourhood in the city centre, once called "Little Dublin", became Montreal's Chinatown. The small Asian community first opened laundries, then restaurants, cafés and other businesses. Today, as the community has spread throughout the city and its suburbs, the majority of Montreal's Chinese residents no longer live here; this Chinatown has become a beautiful tourist "showcase".

UNIFORME DE FACTIONNAIRE
POLICE DE MONTRÉAL

CIRCA 1918 - 1920

MUSÉE DE LA SPVM

1441, rue Saint-Urbain
- Visits by appointment only, Tuesday and Thursday, 9 am to 12 noon
- Tel: 514 280 2043
- Métro: Place-des-Arts or Saint-Laurent

Police stories

The theatre district is home to a rather unusual museum located inside the headquarters of the city police department, at 1441, rue Saint-Urbain. So you'll have to be on your best behaviour as you pass through the metal detector at the entrance. You'll also need to leave your ID in order to get in. Taking such precautions is normal, as visitors get to roam through nine floors of the building, accompanied by a guide, of course.

The police museum was set up in 1992 by a handful of volunteers, most of whom were active or retired police officers and employees of the SPVM (Service de Police de la Ville de Montréal). The museum is dedicated to the history of the officers from the beginnings of the service in 1843 to today.

In their early days the first police corps had only fifty-one members. They didn't wear uniforms until 1848, and they didn't earn the right to bear firearms until 1853.

The guided tour begins on the ground floor with the moving Alley of the Brave, a photo gallery in honour of police officers killed in action. The Boulevard of Heroes is dedicated to the members decorated for outstanding action, such as the bomb disposal expert who defused bombs during the political crisis of October 1970. On each floor, glass display cases stand near the elevator. Inside, you'll find dozens of objects that plunge you into the world of police work, organized by theme: technology, working methods, means of transport, weapons, uniforms, and more. All of these period objects, machines, photographs, and documents are part of our collective memory.

For example, did you know that, in the 1940s, the police ski-patrolled boulevard Pie-IX and avenue du Mont-Royal, and that ice-skating officers kept watch over the city parks as late as 1967, whereas the motorcycle police didn't appear until 1970? All these stories about the police department and its officers are passionately recounted by the volunteer tour guides.

ECONOMUSEUM OF THE VIOLIN

Workshop of luthier Jules Saint-Michel
57, rue Ontario Ouest
• Tel: 514 288 4343 • info@luthiersaintmichel.com
• Métro: Saint-Laurent
• Open Monday to Friday, 2 pm to 5 pm
• Individual admission $8, group visits by appointment

"It'll sing for a lifetime ... and even longer"

What is a string instrument made of? How is a bow made? Who were the great violin-makers of the past? Has Quebec played a role in instrument-making? You'll find the answers to these questions, and hundreds of others, at 57, rue Ontario Ouest, at the workshop of instrument-maker Jules Saint-Michel. Located near Place des Arts and its great venues, the Economuseum of the Violin invites you to plunge into the fascinating world of the violin and other stringed instruments. You'll discover the instrument restoration workshops where skilled artisans perform miracles, a small museum of ancient and contemporary instruments, a resource centre, and, of course, a shop that can pride itself on being the main supplier of Montreal's music schools.

Not just anyone can practice this trade. First of all, you have to love wood and love music, be persevering and skilled with your hands, and have a good ear and an accurate eye. Finally, you need to know how to play the violin, which isn't the easiest skill to acquire.

The guided tours given by the owner are truly fascinating. Jules Saint-Michel, whose given name is Gyula Szentmihaly, was born in Hungary in 1934 and chose to flee his country in 1954 after the Soviet troops invaded to subdue the Hungarian revolution. After spending a few years in Paris studying at the

Sorbonne, he immigrated to Canada in the late 1950s, settling in Montreal where he perfected his instrument-making skills. He began as an apprentice to Montreal luthier Antoine Robichaud, from whom he later took over in the workshops on rue Saint-Denis. He moved his shop to rue Ontario in 1972. Today, he has a team of a dozen or so employees, including his daughter Lilli, his son Claude and his grandson Olivier. Three generations of the Saint-Michel family thus work under the same roof, led by a common passion for this instrument whose shape hasn't changed in 450 years. And, as Antoine Robichaud astutely used to say, a violin, if properly cared for, "will sing for a lifetime ... and even longer".

GODIN BUILDING

2110–2112, boulevard Saint-Laurent
• Métro: Saint-Laurent

Built in 1914 using an innovative approach, in the image of its designer and first owner, architect Joseph-Arthur Godin, this residential block was the first in North America to be built using reinforced concrete. Previously, this technique was used solely for civil engineering structures (bridges, tunnels, aqueducts, etc.).

> *North America's first building in reinforced concrete*

The structure is clearly Art Nouveau in style: the undulation of the façades, the arabesques of the balustrades and the semi-circular balconies are deliberately inspired by the movement that was fashionable in Europe in the early 20th century. The Parisian feel of the ornate wrought-iron balustrades and central spiral staircase, typical of French Second Empire style, adds the finishing touch. The clean lines of the façades, pure geometry of the openings, the absence of adornments and cornices, however, foreshadow the "modern" architecture movement launched in 1919 with the Bauhaus school.

When he began the construction, Godin was the sole owner. That didn't last long, however, as his firm declared bankruptcy before the interior was finished. The building was seized in 1915, thus becoming the property of the Bank of Montreal, which used it as a warehouse. It then passed through the hands of several owners: the Art Nouveau building served as a garment factory and, after the Second World War, as an office building. From 1967 on, boutiques, workshops and lofts shared the space. Over the years, only the interior was modified. In 1990, the Quebec government finally decided to list the Godin Building as a historic monument. In 2003–2004, it was converted into a hotel complex under the direction of architect Dan Hanganu and a new building was added. Its clean, charcoal grey façade is harmoniously integrated with the historic building, thus creating an interesting contrast of black against white. The complex was named the Godin Hotel, in honour of its first owner. In 2007, it changed hands and became the Opus Hotel.

HENRI HENRI, HATTER

189, rue Sainte-Catherine Est
Tel: 514 288 0109 or 1 888 388 0109
• Métro: Berri-UQAM or Saint-Laurent
• Open Monday to Thursday, 10 am to 6 pm, Friday, 10 am to 9 pm,
Saturday and Sunday, 10 am to 5 pm

*A hat
trick!*

At the corner of rue Sainte-Catherine Est and rue Hôtel-de-Ville, the Henri Henri hat shop is an authentic Montreal institution that'll transport you right back to the 1930s. Founded in 1932 by Honorius Henri (hence the shop's name) and Jean-Maurice Lefebvre, this business has always been a family affair. Today, it is managed by Jean-Marc Lefebvre, grandson of the shop's co-founder.

The shop became famous thanks to its enthusiasm for sports, and especially hockey.

In Quebec, when a player scores three goals in a single game, it's called a *tour du chapeau* (from the English "hat trick"). In the 1950s and 1960s, Henri Henri took the expression literally, offering a free hat to every player who completed a hat trick at the Montreal Forum. Famous hockey champion Maurice Richard had quite a collection of them.

Today, the shop no longer gives hats to hockey stars, but several celebrities still figure among its clients: Robert de Niro, Bruce Willis and John Travolta have shopped there, as Marlon Brando and some Montreal mafia bosses did before them.

At Henri Henri's, trying on hats is pure pleasure. They stock all the major brands – Stetson, Biltmore, Borsalino, Mayser and Kango – in a wide variety of sizes. The price of a felt hat ranges from $60 to $750, depending on its quality. You'll also find all sorts of caps: classic peaked caps, newsboys, berets, fishermen's caps and baseball caps. And let's not forget the complementary accessories, so essential to giving your look that final touch: scarves, gloves,

canes, umbrellas, ties, cufflinks, wallets, and more. The shop also offers hat cleaning services. Its lower level is filled with rare tools from another era: wooden forms, moulds and strange steam machines. In short, everything needed to give your ageing headgear a second lease of life.

BUST OF LOUIS-JOSEPH PAPINEAU

The "Franco-Américain" building
1242, rue Saint-Denis
• Métro: Berri-UQAM

> *The hidden head of a Patriots Rebellion hero*

Although passers-by sometimes notice the sculptural group over the entrance to this building at 1242, rue Saint-Denis, few recognize that the head behind it on the left is that of a famous personality. Indeed, it is Louis-Joseph Papineau, hero of the Patriots Rebellion.

But what is this figure doing on the peeling façade of an apartment complex opposite a UQAM building?

When it was built in 1871, this was the home of architect and painter Napoléon Bourassa, who was married to Papineau's daughter, Azélie. Their son, Henri Bourassa, who later founded *Le Devoir* newspaper, grew up in this house.

The sculptures were designed by Napoléon Bourassa himself, but the work was carried out by Louis-Philippe Hébert, Bourassa's young apprentice, who is now considered as one of the greatest Canadian sculptors of the period. The ensemble represents two muses, of sculpture and of painting, on either side of the bust of a woman. Papineau's profile is hidden in the background.

The figure of an old man overhangs the group: it may be a depiction of the celebrated Italian painter and sculptor Leonardo da Vinci. Above the windows of the façade, you'll also find the letters B and P engraved in a decorative style, in reference to the two families Bourassa and Papineau.

Nearly 150 years after its construction, the former Bourassa residence appears to be in a bad way. The building has fallen into oblivion and, with it, the head of this illustrious figure of Canadian history.

ÉMILIE GAMELIN MONUMENT

Place Émilie-Gamelin
Entrance hall of Berri-UQAM métro station north-east of rue Sainte-Catherine

Commuters don't always notice the imposing, 1.9 metre bronze statue at the entrance of Berri-UQAM métro station. It pays tribute to Mother Émilie Gamelin, one of the most remarkable women in Montreal history.

The little sister of the poor

Nicknamed "Providence of the Poor" and "The Prisoners' Angel", Mrs Émilie Tavernier-Gamelin (1800–1851) later became Mother Gamelin and the founder of the Congregation of the Sisters of Providence in 1843. Widowed at the age of 27 and the mother of three children who didn't survive infancy, she was an active woman of character who fought for the destitute and cared for countless victims of the infectious diseases that were rampant at the time. In 1943, she converted a house on rue Sainte-Catherine into a hospice, called the Asile de la Providence (Refuge of Providence). It stood on the very spot where the square bearing her name is located today.

The statue represents this famous Montreal nun in full action, wearing the habit of her sisterhood. Her smile evokes sympathy and openness to humanity, and the basket of food she carries on her arm is destined to alleviate the hunger of the forgotten souls of her time.

In a dynamic manner, the statue has not been placed on a pedestal, but rather on a slope, following the wishes of its creator, Raoul Hunter. The statue thus seems to be approaching passers-by. Indeed, some even come to shake hands with her, as the rubbed-off metal of her outstretched palm suggests.

Created in 2009, the statue was donated to Montreal's Hôtel de Ville (City Hall) by the Congregation of the Sisters of Providence to mark the bicentenary of their founder's birth, in 2000. In fact it was supposed to be erected outside, on the square, but the realistic depiction of the benefactress didn't correspond with Melvin Charney's more modern sculptures. So it was placed at the métro entrance instead. It is one of the two figurative statues displayed in the underground transport network; the other is that of Jacques Cartier in Saint-Henri station.

AN OFTEN MISUNDERSTOOD WORK

Installed on place Émilie Gamelin in 1992 to mark Montreal's 350th anniversary, artist Melvin Charney's work "*Skyscraper, Waterfall, Brooks – A Construction*" is sometimes difficult to understand. It evokes the city and its skyscrapers at the foot of Mont-Royal, from which the groundwater drains into the Saint Lawrence River.

PLAQUE COMMEMORATING 25 YEARS OF THE MONTREAL MÉTRO

Berri-UQAM station

The STM's hidden treasure

Nearly 200,000 people use the Berri-UQAM métro station every day, and nearly 13 million pass through its turnstiles every year. Stuck in their daily routine, few passengers notice a curious bronze plaque set at eye level on one of the red tile walls. Even fewer know of the mini museum hidden behind this plaque. Indeed, in 1991, to celebrate the 25th anniversary of the métro's inauguration, twenty-five STM employees placed twenty-five symbolic objects in a steel box that was later sealed within the concrete. This time capsule won't be opened until October 14, 2016, for the métro's 50th anniversary. Among the objects contained in this little "treasure" box are a $38 monthly pass, a $1.50 single fare ticket, a transfer ticket, a list of all the employees working at the time, a copy of the Equal Employment Opportunities programme, and an operator's tie – a good way to measure inflation and to see if ties from the early 1990s will still be in style twenty-five years later …

WHY ISN'T THERE A LINE 3?

The network has sixty-eight stations and four lines numbered 1 to ... 5: line 3, which was supposed to take the train tracks and tunnel under Mont-Royal towards Cartierville, was never used. Because of Expo 67, line 4, the yellow line leading to Sainte-Hélène and Notre-Dame islands and the South Shore, was used instead.

MONTREAL MÉTRO: HYDRO QUEBEC'S TOP CUSTOMER!

$1,800,000: the amount of the métro's annual electric bill, which makes it Hydro Quebec's top customer. Its electricity consumption could power 10,500 homes.

OTHER SURPRISING FACTS ABOUT THE MONTREAL MÉTRO

The maximum speed of a train is 72 km/h.

98% of passengers arrive at their destination on time or no more than five minutes late. So it's not a good excuse for those late for the office.

The métro has only had to run all night twice in its history. The first time was on March 3, 1971, due to the blizzard of the century, and the second was on December 31, 1999, for the change to year 2000.

A $100 FINE FOR NOT USING THE HANDRAIL

Even with a valid ticket, you can theoretically be fined. Fines of $100 can be issued for "disobeying an order or pictogram", such as carrying a dangerous object or failing to use the escalator handrail.

A PEANUT SMELL?

Mechanical brakes take over from the electrical ones in the last 20 metres of the train's route. They are meant to make the braking easier on the passengers. The cherrywood brake shoes are coated in peanut oil, which creates a rather particular smell when the train brakes at high speed.

FIRST MÉTRO IN THE WORLD TO RUN ENTIRELY ON TYRES

The Montreal métro was the first in the world to run entirely on tyres (nitrogen-filled, with valve). This technique facilitates uphill climbs, starting and braking while reducing noise and the vibrations felt by neighbouring structures.

THE *REFUS GLOBAL* MURAL

Place Paul-Émile Borduas
Quartier Latin, between the Grande Bibliothèque and rue Saint-Denis
• Métro: Berri-UQAM

*A tribute
to Borduas*

I n the past few years a number of murals have brightened up several of the city's neighbourhoods. Few of them, however, have a history as momentous and political as that of place Paul-Émile Borduas.

Inaugurated in 2010 for the 50th anniversary of the death of painter Paul-Émile Borduas, this mural is inspired by the famous *Refus Global* (Total Refusal) manifesto.

The mural, created by graphic designer Thomas Csano and calligrapher Luc Saucier, incorporates visual elements from six of Borduas' paintings. It also includes excerpts from *Refus Global* and other Borduas texts. The word MANIFESTE (manifesto), written vertically in capital letters and in the same style as in the original text, fills the left side of the work. The red birds swarming away, meant to represent the people, symbolize those who signed the manifesto. At the foot of the wall, a bar code illustrates the conformity of a consumer society and the criticism of its "utilitarian spirit".

WHAT WAS THE *REFUS GLOBAL*?

In the 1940s, the authoritarian regime of Premier Maurice Duplessis and the strong influence of the Roman Catholic Church paralysed the freedom of expression of Quebec artists. It was the period known as the *Grande Noirceur* (Great Blackness). In 1948, painter and writer Paul-Émile Borduas, along with fifteen artist-members of the AUTOMATISTE movement, drafted a manifesto that challenged traditional values and rejected the passivity of Quebec society. Four hundred copies of the *Refus Global*, composed of nine texts and several illustrations, were published: they had an explosive effect. The text provides a ruthless description of the society of the time: "We are a small and humble people clutching the robes of priests who've become sole guardians of faith, knowledge, truth and our national heritage; and we have been shielded from the perilous evolution of thought going on all around us, by well-intentioned but misguided educators who distorted the great facts of history whenever they found it impractical to keep us totally ignorant."*

Newspapers, journals and the clergy rejected the text. It wasn't until after Duplessis' death in 1959 that the province began its Quiet Revolution, which lasted from 1960 to 1966.

*From the Ray Ellenwood translation.

OLD MONTREAL, THE ISLANDS

THE GIANTS OF MONTREAL'S CENTRE D'ARCHIVES ❶

Gilles-Hocquart Building
535, avenue Viger Est
• Open Tuesday 9 am to 5 pm; Wednesday, Thursday and Friday 9 am to 9 pm; Saturday and Sunday 9 am to 5 pm; closed Monday
• Tel: 514 873 1100 and 1-800-363-9028 (from Quebec)

Pillars of the early 20th-century economy

Standing proud and majestic at nearly 5 metres high, the "Giants" seem to be enjoying a well-earned retirement in the glass and stone corridor of the former École des Hautes Études Commerciales (HEC) business school.

These statues, created in 1907 by American sculptor Henry Augustus Lukeman to adorn the façade of the Royal Bank of Canada, represented the great bank's contribution to the four pillars of the early 20th-century economy: transport, fishing, industry and agriculture. Each statue bore a symbol of these activities: a locomotive, a trawler and a fish, an oil can (or lamp according to period testimonies), a sheaf of wheat and a maple leaf.

In 1908, the Royal Bank installed its head offices at 147, St-James Street, which later became 221, rue Saint-Jacques. The "Giants" presided over the building's four ionic columns for eight decades. Due to the ravages of time and

weather, they had to be removed during the renovation of the façade in 1991. In the course of this work the transport statue lost a hand. Preservation societies worried that they would be put up for sale on the art market.

Recognized as cultural heritage by the Quebec Ministry of Culture, they finally came into the possession of the Desmarais family (the richest in Quebec) who restored them and donated them to the province's National Archives in 1999. They have been housed in the magnificent Beaux-Arts building of the former HEC ever since.

Entirely renovated by the Dan S. Hanganu architecture firm, the Gilles-Hocquart building is now home to the Montreal Centre d'Archives (guided tours: animation.cam@banq.qc.cq or call 514 873 4300).

REMAINS OF THE OLD FORTIFICATIONS

When you walk through the streets of Old Montreal, it's hard to image that the city was once fortified. However, several traces of these fortifications still remain.

The wooden walls of the first city were replaced in the 18th century by a tall stone wall that ran for 3.5 kilometres and reached a height of 6 metres at some places. With their bastions and curtain walls, Montreal's fortifications formed fourteen defensive fronts containing eight gates and eight posterns. Recent archaeological digs have revealed some remains, and it is now possible to follow the contours of the old walls along a tour of fortified Montreal (see map).

The most spectacular spot is undoubtedly **Champ-de-Mars park**, the only public area that lets you see a section of the original walls built from 1717 to 1744 according to Vauban's principles as developed by the king's chief engineer in New France, Gaspard-Joseph Chaussegros de Léry. Pieces of metal anchored to the stone and connected to the door hanging systems have even been found in two old posterns. Other traces of the fortifications are visible in the **archaeological crypt of the Pointe-à-Callière Museum of Archaeology and History.**

Using a map, you can also follow the many **street markings** in Old Montreal. Granite flagstones mark the site of the old wall and important buildings from the same period. Squares, streets and pavements thus become a kind of treasure hunt into the past. Among the most emblematic sites, from east to west, are **rue de la Commune** with its former military quarters and the king's *canoterie* (boat sheds) where boats were built; **place Jacques-Cartier**, the government stronghold and residence of Governor Vaudreuil; **place Royale**, the city's first public square; and the old general hospital, traces of which can be found on **rue Saint-Pierre** in front of the house of **Mère d'Youville** (see page 77).

ORIENTATION OF NELSON'S COLUMN ❸

Place Jacques-Cartier
• Metro : Champ-de-Mars

A seasick admiral?

Inspired by Trajan's Column in Rome, the famous Nelson's Column in place Jacques-Cartier has a distinctive characteristic: Admiral Nelson, who defeated the French, isn't looking towards the waters of the Saint Lawrence River as might be expected for a seaman, but rather towards the great civil and military institutions of the city at the time: the prison and guardroom, law courts and military parade ground. This curious characteristic is also true of London's column, where the statue faces away from the Thames. One explanation may be that the admiral, great seafaring strategist though he was, suffered from seasickness all his life!

IS NELSON'S COLUMN AN AFFRONT TO THE FRANCOPHONE COMMUNITY?
From the time of its installation, Nelson's Column, a monument to the glory of the English admiral, raised the hackles of the francophone community who saw it as a symbol of British domination. Acting as a sort of counterbalance, a statue of Jean Vauquelin, a French naval officer who participated in the defence of Quebec City in the 18th century, stands on the other side of rue Notre-Dame between the City Hall and the former law courts. Vauquelin thus faces Nelson, defiantly staring back in a constant symbolic battle.

The statue of Nelson that now stands on place Jacques-Cartier is not the original. Worried about the statue's condition, the City of Montreal decided to have it replaced, in 1999, with a copy carved in Indiana limestone, chosen for its sandy colour which closely matched that of the original Coade stone. The original statue is now housed in the Centre d'Histoire de Montréal, on place d'Youville.

THE GOVERNOR'S GARDEN

④

Château Ramezay – historic site and museum
280, rue Notre-Dame Est
• Métro: Champ-de-Mars
• Tel: 514 861 3708 • Admission free

An immersion in New France

If while visiting Old Montreal you just can't take any more of the crowds on place Jacques-Cartier, there's no need to worry. Escape is nearby at 280, rue Notre-Dame Est.

Behind Château Ramezay, which stands opposite the City Hall, you'll find a small French-style garden accessible at all times. Just take the short rue le Royer Est off place Jacques-Cartier.

This haven of peace, known as the Ramezay Museum gardens or the Governor's garden, was renovated in 2000 following the original design. The Governor of Trois-Rivières, then of Montreal from 1704 to his death in 1724 (with the exception of the period from 1714 to 1716 when he served as acting Governor of New France), Claude de Ramezay chose to have his home built on the small hill of rue Notre-Dame. His 4,200 square metre property comprised a vegetable garden, orchard and a pleasure garden. Due to urban

expansion, the Governor's garden only covers 750 square metres today, but its style and content still reflect the life led by the 18th-century Montreal nobility.

This garden "à la française" is organized exactly as it was when the Governor lived here, with three equal sections framed on three sides by walls, at the foot of which aromatic and medicinal herbs grow. A fountain ornamented by a bronze goat's head illustrates the important role that wells played in such period gardens. In the vegetable garden, you'll find vegetables with a long shelf life that had to provide sustenance for the colonists throughout the winter: cabbage, pumpkins, carrots, turnips, peas, beans, onions and the very popular Jerusalem artichokes and cucumbers. Medicinal and aromatic plants are omnipresent. The former were believed to be more effective than the doctor and were even used to chase away demons, while the latter were quite useful for masking odours, given the relative lack of cleanliness of the time …

The refinement of the nobility can be seen in the varieties rarely found in 18th-century Quebec, such as the artichoke and asparagus. The fruit trees in the orchard are really at home here. They are protected with straw in winter. The apple and plum trees are flourishing, as are the grape vines, but the pear and peach trees have more trouble adjusting to the climate.

As for the central pleasure garden, it is an illustration of how the appreciation of flowers had spread through nearly all classes of French Canadian society. It is easy to imagine the beautiful receptions once held here by the Governor, especially during the summer historic activities hosted by the museum. The château café overlooking the garden is also home to one of the city's most beautiful terraces.

CLIMBING THE NOTRE-DAME-DE-BON-SECOURS BELL TOWER

Musée Marguerite Bourgeoys - Notre-Dame-de-Bon-Secours Chapel
400, rue Saint-Paul Est
- Métro: Champ-de-Mars • Tel: 514 282 8670
- Open Tuesday to Sunday; closed mid-January to late February
- March and April: 11 am to 3:30 pm
- May to Thanksgiving (Canada): 10 am to 5:30 pm
- Thanksgiving (Canada) to mid-January: 11 am to 3:30 pm

> *The most beautiful view of the Old Port*

With her arms outstretched over the Saint Lawrence River, the monumental sculpture of Notre-Dame-de-Bon-Secours towers over Montreal's Old Port, extending her protection to all the sailors arriving in the city. Few know that you can climb all the way up to the pinnacle that supports her to enjoy a one-off view. To get there, visit the Marguerite Bourgeoys Museum, which covers more than 2,000 years of Quebec history in its seven exhibition rooms and chapel, and then climb up to the pinnacle, a veritable observation tower. Here, it is easy to imagine the Montreal of yesteryear with its river, forest, wooden fort and early homes.

NEARBY

THE CITY HALL BALCONY WHERE GENERAL DE GAULLE GAVE HIS SPEECH

It was from the balcony of the Montreal City Hall, on July 24, 1967, that French President de Gaulle gave an impromptu speech which he ended with these famous words which would cause such uproar: "Long live Montreal! Long live Quebec! Long live French Canada! And long live France!" The president thus set off a serious political crisis between Canada and France as he seemed to support the Quebec sovereignty movement, whose slogan was precisely "*Vive le Québec libre!*" (Long live free Quebec!). Incidentally, this event focused the world's attention on this francophone province.

"LES CHUCHOTEUSES" SCULPTURE

Rue Saint-Paul (corner of rue Saint-Dizier)
• Métro: Place-d'Armes

These three buxom women, who seem to have jumped out of a Botero painting, are so absorbed by their conversation that they ignore the passers-by who sometimes stop and stare. This bronze sculpture by artist Rose-Aimée Bélanger is called *Les Chuchoteuses* (The Gossipers).

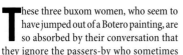

Conversation on the square

To see them, take rue Saint-Paul towards the east; the work has been installed in a small recess where rue Saint-Paul crosses rue Saint-Dizier. This forgotten space was officially named place Saint-Dizier in 2006, when this sculpture was unveiled.

Despite their massive appearance, the "*chuchoteuses*", with their identical hairstyles and dress, emanate sensuality and flightiness.

Rose-Aimée Bélanger, Quebec native and francophone artist, lives in northern Ontario and sculpts in clay; her works are then cast in bronze. Her plump female subjects tell a story. Their faces express three emotions, which are reinforced by the placement of their hands: one is eloquent while the other two listen a bit dubiously. You can't help but wonder what they're talking about. Indeed, people strolling through Old Montreal often stop to join these three gossips and snap a memorable photo.

Rue Saint-Paul, which runs parallel to rue Notre-Dame, was one of Montreal's first streets. It follows the banks of the Saint Lawrence River, which thus makes it one of the few curved streets of this North American metropolis. The street ends at the centre of place Royale, where the local market was held until 1803. For many years, it was an important commercial district before becoming the home of the Montreal press in the 19th century: the offices of a dozen political and literary newspapers and magazines lined the street. This bustling district was also the first to be equipped with oil lamps for street lighting.

NEARBY

RUELLE CHAGOUAMIGON

Further west on rue Saint-Paul, on the left you'll find ruelle Chagouamigon, which leads to rue de la Capitale. The shady alley, a reminder of the early days of Montreal, was given this American Indian name in the 17th century in reference to a trading post opened by the explorers Radisson and Desgroseillers.

At the time, two other lanes with American Indian names – Michilimakinac and Outaouaise – were once located in this lively district. The entire neighbourhood bustled noisily during the fur-trading days, so much so, in fact, that one street earned the nickname "hell street".

COURS LE ROYER

- Métro: Place-d'Armes

*An oasis
of tranquility
and freshness*

Cours le Royer, between boulevard Saint-Laurent and rue Saint-Sulpice, is a real haven of peace just a step away from Notre-Dame Basilica and its lively square. It's the perfect spot for a secluded lunch break.

In summer, the fountains create an ambiance of cool freshness and relaxation in this street with an unusual past that has been closed to traffic since 1982.

In the mid-19th century, the city experienced an economic boom and decided to encourage commercial activity in the old city. Consequently, the religious community the Hospitalières de l'Hôtel-Dieu de Montréal (Montreal Hospital) decided to move their hospital to a healthier and quieter place to the north. In 1861, the community began having rental warehouses built on the site of the former Hôtel-Dieu. Three new streets were created, including rue le Royer in homage to Jérôme le Royer de la Dauversière, the man behind the missionary project that marked the birth of Ville-Marie (Montreal). He had set up and financed the small colony directed by Paul Chomedey de Maisonneuve and Jeanne Mance, the two official co-founders of the city. Without le Royer, Montreal would undoubtedly never have seen the light of day in 1642.

In the 20th century, the 1861–1872 warehouses were gradually converted into apartments and offices. The street became a garden area in the 1980s, to the great delight of pedestrians.

NEARBY

BAS-RELIEF OF MARGUERITE BOURGEOYS

2, rue le Royer

In 1925, the Salada Tea Company commissioned a sculpture of Marguerite Bourgeoys that was incorporated into the façade on rue le Royer.

The company thus emphasizes the role of the woman who founded the Congregation of Notre-Dame. It was on this site that, on April 30, 1659, Marguerite Bourgeoys taught her first class in the city's first school, which was set up in a stable at the corner of rue Saint-Paul and rue Saint-Dizier.

MUSÉE DE LA BANQUE DE MONTRÉAL   ❽

129, rue Saint-Jacques
- Tel: 514 877 6810
- Métro: Place-d'Armes
- Open Monday to Friday, 10 am to 4 pm
- Admission free

*Basilica
of business*

The tiny museum of the Bank of Montreal is located at 129, rue Saint-Jacques in the connecting passage between the bank's main branch (a majestic neoclassical structure built in 1847) and its headquarters, built in 1960. This unique museum dates back to the origins of the finance industry.

Founded in 1817, the Bank of Montreal is the oldest banking institution in Canada and it has preserved its rich and historic heritage. When you enter the museum, you find yourself standing in front of a startlingly detailed reconstitution of the bank's first office, complete with iron bars. An interesting collection of coins and banknotes – the first issued in Canada, even before the Bank of Canada was established in 1935 – is displayed in the showcases, along with period documents and accessories, photographs and a collection of money boxes. In the corridor, the four terracotta panels depicting agriculture, navigation, arts and crafts, and commerce are the bas-reliefs that once graced the façade of the bank's first building, inaugurated in 1819 then later replaced by a post office.

A visit to the museum is above all a chance to discover this historic building that still serves the clients of the Montreal branch. The elegant neo-Gothic structure, designed by local architect John Wells as a manifestation of the city's financial power in the mid-19th century, was in a modest way inspired

by the Pantheon of Rome, with a dome to counterbalance the six Corinthian columns of the portico. On the pediment by Scottish sculptor John Steell, installed in 1867, are the symbols of Canada: the bank's coat of arms flanked by two American Indians and, on the sides, a sailor and a colonist symbolizing commerce and economic prosperity. The work, which is 15.8 metres long and weighs 25 tonnes, was completed in Scotland before being shipped over in several pieces. This exterior façade was the only section to be preserved when the bank's premises were extended between 1901 and 1905.

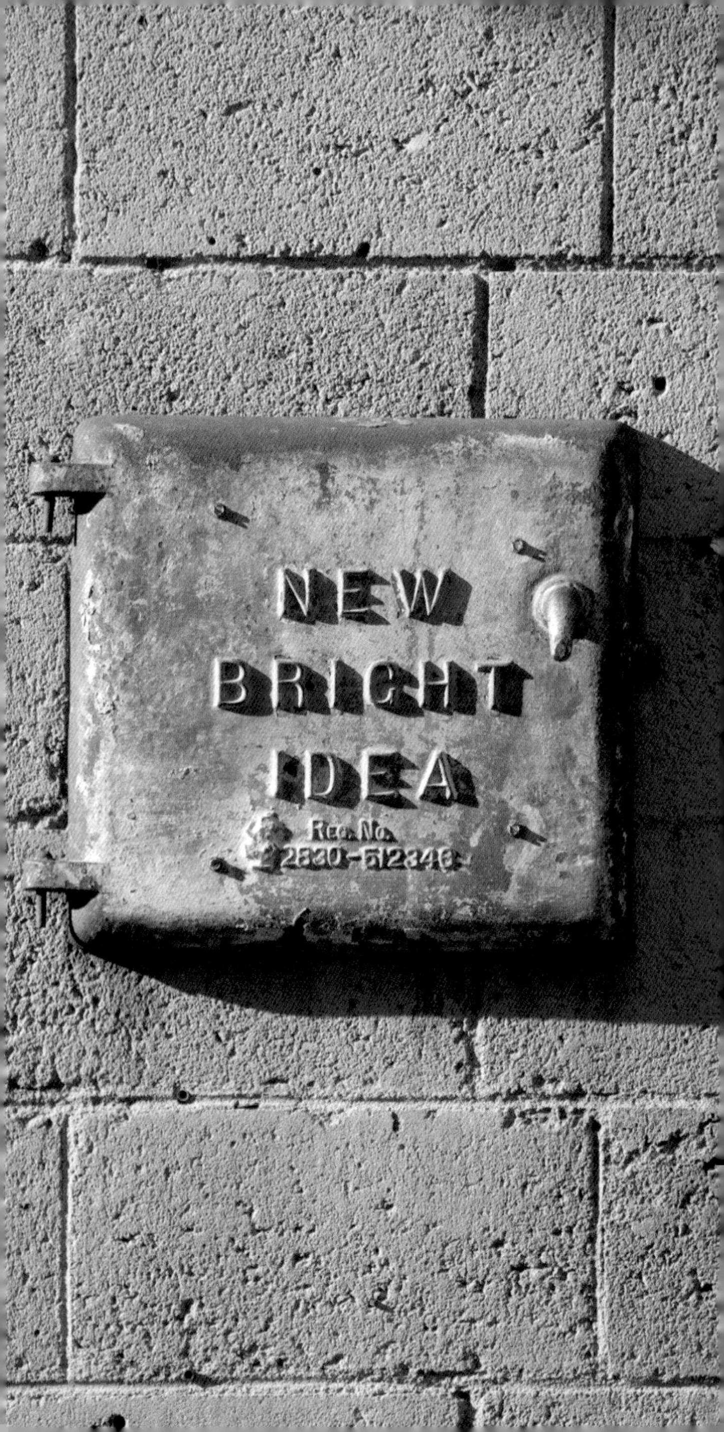
NEW
BRIGHT
IDEA
Reg. No.
2830-512348

THE "NEW BRIGHT IDEA" PLAQUE ⑨

408–410, rue Saint-François-Xavier, corner of rue Saint-Éloi
• Métro: Place-d'Armes or Square-Victoria

> *A souvenir of "Magasin Hutchison"*

At 408–410, rue Saint-François-Xavier, at the corner of rue Saint-Éloi, the "NEW BRIGHT IDEA" plaque is the only sign on the façade of the popular Le Garde-Manger restaurant. It's a reminder of the former purpose of this site: the restaurant didn't move into this nearly 200-year-old structure until 2006, deciding to use the former tenant's classic chandeliers and old wooden furniture to decorate the dining room.

Built in 1845 by the widow of William Hutchison (hence the name Magasin Hutchison) and her second husband, William Lunn, the building served as both store and home. For most of its existence it has kept this double purpose as merchants and manufacturers succeeded one another to the present day.

Chuck Hughes, Le Garde-Manger's chef, was cleaning out the basement soon after he moved in when he discovered an old boiler with a trapdoor bearing cast-iron letters that spelled out the phrase "NEW BRIGHT IDEA", probably some manufacturer's slogan. He immediately decided to use it as the only embellishment on the façade along with the street number, which he also made using materials recuperated from the house: some original numbers (4 and 0) and machine parts (8).

A PIECE OF THE BERLIN WALL

Ruelle des Fortifications
World Trade Centre of Montreal
Entrances at 747, rue Square-Victoria; 393, rue Saint-Jacques; 380,
rue Saint-Antoine; and on rue Saint-Pierre
• Métro: Square-Victoria

A surprise gift

The history of ruelle des Fortifications is closely linked to that of two very different walls.

In 1717, extensive construction works were begun to replace the wooden stockade that had protected the city since 1685. The new stone wall, completed in the 1730s, was meant to provide the city with better defences, even if only temporary. At the end of the 18th century, not only had the walls become outdated, given the increasing use of heavy artillery, but they were also constricting the ever-growing city. The inhabitants demanded that they be demolished, and they were, between 1804 and 1812. The ruelle des Fortifications replaced a section of the wall between rue McGill and rue Saint-Laurent.

In the following century, this once residential neighbourhood became a financial district. As it ran parallel to rue Saint-Jacques with its banks, this alley was used as a service road for the surrounding buildings.

When the World Trade Centre of Montreal was built from 1987 to 1992, a section of ruelle des Fortifications was preserved and covered with a large glass ceiling, thus creating a vast atrium that was then filled with stores and restaurants.

In 1991, a curious package arrived at the port of Montreal. It was a surprise gift from the city of Berlin for the 350th anniversary of the founding of Montreal, which was to be celebrated the following year. This piece of the Berlin Wall which fell, along with the rest, on November 9, 1989 at the Brandenburg Gate, weighs 2.5 tonnes and is 3.6 metres high and 1.2 metres wide. It took the city three years to find a place to display it. As none of the Montreal museums wanted it, and the idea of displaying it outdoors was rejected for reasons of security and preservation, the World Trade Centre decided to make a home for it in the covered alleyway where the city's stone wall had once stood just over two centuries earlier.

NEARBY

A FOUNTAIN ON THE MOVE

This large fountain where newly-wed couples like to have their picture taken is dominated by a statue of Amphitrite, wife of the god Poseidon, an imposing figure of Greek mythology. The story behind this monument is original. The statue comes from the small town of Saint-Mihiel in the Meuse department of north-east France. Dismantled then kept in storage for many years, this sculpture by artist Dieudonné Barthélémy Guibal dating from around 1755 was listed in the sales catalogue of a Parisian antique dealer. In 1990, Paul Desmarais senior, a Quebec businessman, bought it to decorate the fountain that his company, the Power Corporation, had already commissioned.

GAS LAMPS ON RUE SAINTE-HÉLÈNE ⑪

• Métro: Square-Victoria

T hanks to its unique ambiance, this little street in the Old Montreal district has become a favourite for crews filming period movies.

19th-century lighting

Indeed, in 1998, as part of one of the first implementations of the Lighting Plan, rue Sainte-Hélène was once again lit as it had been in the past – by twenty-two gas lamps. What a beautiful way to highlight the architecture for which this street is renowned.

Opened in 1818 on the former property of the Récollet monks, at the same time as rue le Moyne and rue des Récollets, rue Sainte-Hélène grew considerably in importance from 1858 to 1871, as it became home to a dozen stores, warehouses and other commercial buildings. To impress their clients, the shopkeepers didn't skimp on style, which resulted in the street's remarkable architectural homogeneity. The street has managed to preserve its appearance over time, even if a luxury hotel and offices have gradually replaced the wholesale dealers.

"ILLUMINATION TOUR"

At nightfall, rue Sainte-Hélène becomes part of the "Illumination Tour", which was inspired by the Festival of Lights in Lyon, France, Montreal's sister city. Indeed, experts from both cities collaborated to highlight the architectural elements of certain buildings and streets in Old Montreal using strategically placed lighting. Visitors can thus follow a 90 minute tour leading through place Jacques-Cartier, place d'Armes, place Royale, place d'Youville, rue de la Commune, rue Saint-Paul, rue Saint-Pierre and rue Sainte-Hélène. The City Hall, Bonsecours market, Notre-Dame Basilica, Saint James Hotel, Saint Paul Hotel and Pointe-à-Callière Museum figure among the illuminated buildings and monuments – and more are added to the list every year.

THE OLD YOUVILLE STABLES ⑫

300/310, place d'Youville
• Métro: Square-Victoria

*Not
a horse's tail
in sight!*

In the 19th century, this square named after Saint Marguerite of Youville was a centre of Montreal business life. It's difficult to miss the former Bouthillier warehouses, known as the Écuries d'Youville (Youville Stables), with their beautiful façade of grey stone ornamented with two *oeil-de-boeuf* windows. Once you pass under the arched entrance with its wrought-iron gate, you find yourself in a perfectly restored and quite charming courtyard – a pleasant spot for a break between meetings in summer.

In fact, there were never any stables here: the name comes from the property development company Les Écuries d'Youville Ltd that bought these warehouses in 1967.

On a property leased from the Grey Nuns, potash wholesaler Jean Bouthillier and his son Louis-Tancrède had three warehouses built from 1827 to 1828 to store this precious powder produced by burning hardwoods (maple, oak) and used to fix colours on printed cotton and to manufacture glass and soap. At the time, along with timber and grain, potash was one of the major exports to transit through Montreal port. The warehouses then passed through the hands of several tenants. After a grain and flour merchant came the Ogilvie & Co flour mill, which occupied the site for over twenty years. Next, there was a customs broker, followed by a company specializing in dairy equipment and supplies, which stayed until 1961. After a period of inactivity, the nuns sold the property and the warehouses were reconverted into offices, flats and a famous restaurant.

HOSPITAL OF THE GREY NUNS

138, rue Saint-Pierre
• Métro: Square-Victoria • Visits by appointment, call 514 842 9411
• Open daily 9:30 am to 11:30 am and 1:30 pm to 4 pm; closed
Monday • Admission free

*In
the house
of Mère d'Youville*

Marguerite d'Youville, the founder of the Sisters of Charity who was canonized in 1990, took over the direction of Montreal's first general hospital in 1747, fifty years after it was built by the Frères Charon (from 1693 to 1697).

The hospital served the poor and the rejected. "Go see the Grey Nuns. They never turn anyone away," people used to say. Marguerite lived in the General Hospital until her death on December 23, 1771.

Of the original buildings, only one wing and the ruins of the chapel remain. The guided tour is led by one of the last sisters still living here. You can walk on the dining room's original stone floor, admire the main foyer and the gargoyle sink. On the upper floor, a permanent exhibit recounts the main events of Marguerite d'Youville's life.

Afterwards, you religiously enter the room where the mother of the poor prayed and later passed away. A section of the original wooden flooring has been preserved. The sister's presence is evoked in all simplicity by a prie-Dieu and the figure of Christ on the Cross. This moving visit ends in the small shaded garden that surrounds the statue of Marguerite.

WHY ARE THEY CALLED GREY NUNS?

The Sisters of Charity are also called the Grey Nuns (*Sœurs Grises* in French) because of the grey habit they wear as a sign of humility, but also as a reminder of Marguerite d'Youville's past. She had married an egotistical and untrustworthy man who damaged her reputation by illegally selling alcohol, known for getting the American Indians drunk (*griser* in French).

THE TUGBOAT DANIEL MCALLISTER

Basin of Lock 1 on Lachine Canal
Along the Montreal Old Port promenade
At the foot of rue McGill
• Métro: Square-Victoria

Tugboats are the guardian angels of the waters, working in ports, on rivers, in the Great Lakes and the seas and oceans of the world. These small but very powerful and manoeuvrable boats serve to guide, tow and push big ships. They play a crucial role in helping them to navigate ports and difficult passages.

Been around for a century

The tugboat Daniel McAllister is a veteran. It is Canada's largest tugboat and the world's second oldest ocean-going tugboat.

Originally christened Helena, it began its career in 1907 on the Atlantic coast before moving to the Great Lakes region. The owner took the opportunity to update it, replacing its steam engine with a much more powerful diesel motor. In 1956, after another "facelift", the tugboat was renamed Helen MB. The company McAllister Towing Limited brought the tugboat to Montreal in the 1960s and rechristened it a final time, naming it after one of the members of this maritime family. It finished its long career in the port of Montreal before retiring in the 1980s.

The tug probably would have been dismantled if the Musée Maritime de Québec hadn't acquired it in 1997, thus fulfilling its mission to preserve, study and promote maritime heritage. The following year, it was placed in the capable hands of the Old Port of Montreal Corporation, which undertook restoration work to return it to its former glory. The exteriors of the tug and its rowboat were repaired and repainted in their original colours, the woodwork and vessel identification plates were restored, as were the portholes, navigation lights and searchlights. It was treated as a museum piece, which is exactly what it is!

THE GOLDEN AGE OF MONTREAL'S OLD PORT

The port as we know it today is the result of major development work undertaken in the early 20th century.

From 1896 to 1930, it served as the connection between transatlantic ships and the trains heading to or from all of North America. Millions of tonnes of merchandise passed through Montreal. To deal with all this traffic, the port had to modernize its facilities. Grain elevators, warehouses and over a kilometre of quays were built. Traces of this prosperous period can still be seen in the Old Port today.

SURFING ON THE SAINT LAWRENCE

Between Sainte-Hélène and Notre-Dame islands
Between Cité-du-Havre and Notre-Dame

> *On the river, you can surf as far as you want!*

The water may be colder than in Australia, but there aren't any sharks! Who would believe that you can go surfing right in the Cité-du-Havre, opposite the Port of Montreal?

In fact it's river surfing, a relatively new but rapidly growing sport. Like traditional surfing, you paddle out to the wave before standing on your board. The difference is that, on the ocean, you ride until the wave breaks while, on the river, you can ride as far as you want, or as far as you can! The advantage is that surfers no longer have to wait for the perfect wave. Instead, it's the waves that wait for the surfers. When you stay in one spot, it's much easier to find your balance and control your turns and tricks. So on the river, a beginner can improve without having to confront large ocean waves.

Montreal's "spot" is just behind Habitat 67, the group of avant-garde homes by architect Moshe Safdie, Cité du Havre.

This permanent wave is caused by a ditch dug during the construction of Île Notre-Dame for Expo 67. The workers needed more backfill, so a dyke was built, allowing them to drag the riverbed. When enough material had been extracted, the dyke was demolished but the ditch remained, creating this famous wave.

At certain times of the year, depending on the water level, the wave is bigger and attracts more surfers who gather on the riverbanks. So sometimes you have to wait a while for your turn.

More experienced surfers go to Lachine rapids, further downstream on the Saint Lawrence. Watch out: its many obstacles and whirlpools make this a dangerous spot. The rapids are also used for white-water kayaking, rafting, jet boating and jet-ski excursions.

THE CHINESE RAPIDS

In 1535, Frenchman Jacques Cartier was the first European to sail up the Saint Lawrence River "to the Iroquois village of Hochelaga" (Montreal). Upstream from the city, he couldn't get past the rapids, which were later mockingly called the Lachine rapids to make fun of the explorers who thought this route was leading them to China (*La Chine* in French).

THE EIFFEL TOWERS OF JACQUES-CARTIER BRIDGE

16

• Métro: Jean-Drapeau

An urban legend

There's an urban legend about the famous bridge over the Saint Lawrence River and, more precisely, about the metal structures that dominate its main span. Legend says that it was France that gave these four Eiffel Tower-shaped finials to Montreal.

But this legend is unfounded and is, in fact, a mix-up with the bust of Jacques Cartier, which *was* a gift from France (see below).

From the roadway, it is difficult to appreciate that each of these finials stands nearly 4 metres tall and weighs around 6 tonnes. They tower over the bridge and the city at a height of over 100 metres. Luckily, the steel fitters who came to restore the bridge in the summer of 2010 weren't afraid of heights!

WHEN FRANCE DONATED A BUST OF JACQUES CARTIER

In 1934, when Montreal Harbour Bridge was renamed due to public pressure and became Jacques-Cartier Bridge, France donated a bust of the famous French explorer, thus also marking the 400th anniversary of the discovery of Canada.

Today, the bust is displayed on a wall next to the Île Sainte-Hélène pavilion, just before the access ramp to the island.

THE BRIDGE'S TREASURE

When the cornerstone of the bridge was laid in 1926, a time capsule with fifty-nine objects was placed in pile 26, at the corner of rue Notre-Dame and rue Saint-Antoine.

Yet today, nobody knows exactly where this "treasure" lies. It supposedly holds a jumbled assortment of newspapers from August 7, 1926, coins (including a gold one), three aerial photographs of the port of Montreal, maps, annual reports and other period documents.

ROSE GARDEN OF THE HÉLÈNE DE CHAMPLAIN RESTAURANT

200, chemin du Tour-de-l'Isle, Île Sainte-Hélène
• Métro: Jean-Drapeau
• Free access

Roses and an American Indian village

Not far from the Floralies Gardens, you can also admire the magnificent roses in the garden of the famous Hélène de Champlain restaurant, at 200, chemin du Tour-de-l'Isle on Île Sainte-Hélène.

Converted in 1955, the former 1937 Sports Pavilion, with its sloping roof and dormer windows, resembles typical Quebec homes. For the 1967 International and Universal Exposition (Expo 67), the restaurant was converted into a pavilion of honour to host dignitaries and heads of state. A rose garden was planted according to the plans of landscape designer Louis Perron. The Montreal-Lakeshore Rotary Club graciously provided the thousands of rose bushes in commemoration of the centenary of the Canadian Confederation. Serving as an intimate extension of the pavilion, the rose garden has preserved its general original structure and continues to exude thousands of subtle fragrances today.

In 2004, archaeological digs revealed traces of an American Indian village north of the rose garden. Nearly 250 objects, including pottery, hand-cut stone tools, pipes and animal bones, clearly indicated the presence of the Iroquois on the island as early as 1000 BC.

NEARBY

THE ISLAND'S OLD MILITARY CEMETERY
Established outside the fort (now the Stewart Museum) in 1848, this small cemetery was used until 1869.

The tombs were exhumed in 1915. Today, nothing remains of the original tombs, except for a commemorative monument inaugurated in 1935 that bears the names of those who were once laid to rest here.

TERRACE OF THE TOUR DE LÉVIS

At the heart of Île Sainte-Hélène
• Tel: 514 872 9013
• Métro: Jean-Drapeau

A breathtaking view

Located on one of the little mounds of Île Sainte-Hélène, the imposing Tour de Lévis looks as if it were once part of Montreal's old fortifications, designed to push back a possible Iroquois, English or American invasion. This isn't the case, however, and the truth is much less exciting. In fact, it's nothing more than a water tower built in 1936 to supply the island's hydraulic system.

The architecture of the stone-built tower, 30 metres high, is none the less remarkable. Inside, 157 steps lead up to an observation deck that provides a breathtaking 360° view. You can see the Saint Lawrence River, the city and, on clear days, the foothills of Montérégie to the south. In autumn, when the surrounding treetops take on colours of an Indian summer, you're so close to the blazing canopy that you feel part of it.

The entirely restored tower can now be hired from May to October for lunches, unforgettable evenings, or during the Montreal Fireworks Festival held nearby in La Ronde. The terrace can accommodate up to sixty people from 11 am until late in the evening.

FLORALIES GARDENS

• Métro: Jean-Drapeau

In the shadow of the Formula 1 track

Every year, hundreds of thousands of spectators crowd onto Île Notre-Dame to watch the famous Formula 1 Grand Prix race on the Gilles Villeneuve track. Just a short distance away lies a magnificent garden that had its hour of glory when it was created in 1980 for the Montreal International Flower Show.

What a striking contrast they make: the deafening sound of the cars on one hand, and, on the other, the Olympian calm of these quiet gardens rarely visited by tourists.

In 1980, the greatest landscape architects from twenty-five countries met in Montreal for the first flower shows organized in North America. For the occasion, a section of the Expo 67 grounds were redesigned. The flower show covered nearly 16 hectares.

Today, roughly 5 hectares of exceptional flower gardens remain; over time, they have gained in both maturity and beauty.

Nestled in this oasis of tranquility opposite the city centre skyscrapers, the gardens feature more than 100,000 annual plants and 5,000 shrubs, including some extremely rare varieties. Charming little canals flow through this luxurious environment, over a total distance of 1.5 kilometres. Every year from late June to late August, the pedal boats work their charm below the Rialto Bridge, the Madonna Bridge and the Bridge of Sighs. You can also enjoy a picnic in the shade of a magnificent weeping willow tree while watching the birds frolic on the canal and the fish swim beneath the ripples.

The gardens are easily accessible by bike via Victoria Bridge and the seaway cycle path, the Jacques-Cartier Bridge and the Concorde Bridge, or, in summer, by the river shuttle from Longueuil or Montreal's Old Port (kids love it). By foot, the Jean-Drapeau métro station is, as they say here, just a "nice short walk" away – meaning a quarter-hour walk.

THE KWAKIUTL TOTEM POLE

Floralies Gardens
Île Sainte-Hélène
• Métro: Jean-Drapeau

> *The only trace of Expo 67's Indians of Canada Pavilion*

You have probably heard of the fabulous collection of totem poles in Vancouver's Stanley Park, but Montreal also has its American Indian totem pole. It's the only remaining trace of the Indians of Canada Pavilion built for the International and Universal Exposition of 1967.

Made from red cedar, the almost 20 metre tall Kwakwaka'wakw (or Kwakiutl) totem pole stands in Floralies Gardens on Île Sainte-Hélène. The totem pole, a tradition among the American Indian tribes of North America's north-west coast, depicts both familiar and mythical animals that illustrate belonging to a family or a clan. At the top of Montreal's pole sits the raven, the bird of thunder, who, like Zeus, controls lightning. Next comes a bear, followed by a sisiutl, a mythical two-headed sea serpent, a killer whale devouring a seal, a beaver and, at the bottom, a tribal chief. These six figures represent the emblems of several clans working together.

A traditional art form of the Kwakiutl nation, an American Indian tribe of British Columbia, this totem pole was carved in the late 1960s by Henry Hunt and his son Tony for Expo 67. It was repaired and repainted in 2007 according to Kwalkiutl tradition, which stipulates that the restoration must be done by members of the original sculptor's family. This custom preserves the heritage of the ancestors while encouraging the transmission of skills from generation to generation.

American Indians are believed to have inhabited the island of Montreal since at least 8000 BC. Archaeological digs on Île Sainte-Hélène in 2003 revealed ceramics dating from 1200 to 1350, which proves the presence of American Indians under the present-day Jacques-Cartier Bridge.

INUIT MURAL OF THE CANADIAN PAVILION

1, circuit Gilles-Villeneuve, on Île Notre-Dame
• Tel: 514 872 9013
• Métro: Jean-Drapeau

*A legacy
of Expo 67*

At the time, in 1967, it was a first: the completion of a large-scale mural by Inuit artists on the occasion of the International Exposition. Inuit art was finally introduced to the world and numerous sculptures were displayed in La Toundra restaurant in the Canadian Pavilion. The country commissioned two artists from the village of Cape Dorset to complete a work composed of several wall paintings entitled *The Arctic World*. Kumakuluk Saggiak and Elijah Pootoogook, both recognized artists today, used a technique inspired by Italian sgraffito: first the wall is coated with a thin layer of plaster about 2.5 centimetres thick, then covered with a layer of dark grey paint. Next, the motifs of the work are drawn. For the large mural depicting the village of Cape Dorset, the artists removed the surface around each element so that the drawing stood out in black on white. For the other frescoes, they engraved directly into the surface, creating a white design on the black background. Certain sections show use of both methods.

Thus, traditional hunting and fishing scenes juxtapose the depiction of the village of Cape Dorset, composed of houses and buildings built by the white people. The arrival of technology (hydroplanes and snowmobiles) is already visible. For the visitors, the majority of whom were discovering Inuit art for the first time, this mural was a real plunge into the daily life of these Arctic communities that were gradually overwhelmed by European civilization.

Officially named "Katimavik", the Canadian Pavilion is one of the buildings that survived after the Expo. The immense inverted pyramid and its concert hall, which once sat on the building's white roof, are gone. Available to hire, La Toundra restaurant hosts receptions, weddings, business meetings and other events, thus offering the opportunity to rediscover these magnificent murals.

SAINT-LAURENT,
SAINT-DENIS, PLATEAU

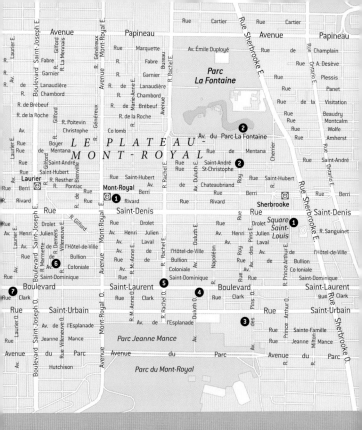

sept heures et demie du matin métro de Montréal
c'est plein d'immigrants
ça se lève de bonne heure
ce monde-là

vieux cœur de la ville
battrait-il donc encore
grâce à eux

vieux cœur usé de la ville
avec ses spasmes
ses embolies
ses souffles au cœur
tous ses défauts

toutes les raisons du monde qu'il aurai
s'arrêter
renoncer

GÉRALD GODIN'S "TANGO DE MONTRÉAL" ❶

4443, rue Rivard (side overlooking place Gérald-Godin)
• Métro: Mont-Royal

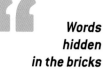

*Words
hidden
in the bricks*

Every day, hundreds of people wait for the bus at the stop behind Mont-Royal métro station without even noticing that the large brick façade on the other side of the street conceals a famous poem from Quebecker literature. Inaugurated in 1999, the work was designed as part of the redevelopment of the square around the métro entrance, which led to the creation of place Gérald-Godin, named after the Quebec poet and deputy. "Tango de Montréal" was published in 1983 as part of the poet's *Sarzènes* collection. The designers of the square decided to engrave it on a façade in response to another well-known poem, by Michel Bujold, which had previously been engraved on Gérald Godin's house. A highly symbolic gesture …

NEARBY

PHONETIC POEM "LETTRE À JEAN DRAPEAU"

336, rue du Square Saint-Louis
• Métro: Sherbrooke

You have to go round the left side of the house at 336, rue du Square

Saint-Louis, the former home of poet and politician Gérald Godin and his paramour, singer Pauline Julien, to find this rather unusual mural. Is it in a foreign language? Well, not really. It's a phonetic poem: you have to read it aloud to understand it. Written by Michel Bujold, who describes himself as a poet-designer-entertainer, this "Lettre à Jean Drapeau" dates from 1975 and has been miraculously preserved. Square Saint-Louis, often called carré Saint-Louis, has been a privileged witness to Montreal's cultural history, as it has been home to numerous artists over the years: Émile Nelligan, Gaston Miron, Denise Boucher, Gérald Godin, Pauline Julien, André Gagnon, and, more recently, Michel Tremblay, Gilles Carle and Dany Laferrière.

LES LEÇONS SINGULIÈRES ❷

Place Roy on rue Roy, between rue Saint-André and rue Saint-Christophe, and in La Fontaine Park
• Métro: Sherbrooke

> *These chairs aren't made for sitting*

When it first appeared on the small place Roy in the Plateau Mont-Royal district, the work *Les Leçons Singulières*, dreamt up by sculptor Michel Goulet, provoked strong reactions. What was the point of these chairs if you couldn't sit on them?

In the years that followed, the installation was vandalized numerous times – a chair was even stolen in 1995. As a precautionary measure, the city removed all the chairs from the place Roy sculptural group, leaving the site empty for over a year. In 1999, the sculptures were reinstalled with a new anchoring system, the missing chair was replaced with an identical copy, and two new chairs – ones you can actually sit on – were added.

The stolen chair was recovered twelve years later, in 2007 – a rare occurrence. The artist eventually decided to place it in the centre of a new public work, *Un Jardin à Soi*, unveiled in 2011 in the Botanical Garden arboretum.

Today, *Les Leçons Singulières* is composed of two *volets*, or sculptural groups. The first, on place Roy, includes a brass table-fountain depicting a map of the world where you'll find the five continents taking a swim, and eight chairs, six of which are marked with a distinctive symbol: house, spiral, wheels, labyrinth, funnel and puzzle. The second *volet* is 300 metres away in La Fontaine Park, at the Léo Ayotte viewpoint. It comprises a relief sculpture-map of the park and six chairs arranged in a curve along the balustrade. The artist has placed objects relating to the activities practiced here in the park under each chair: trainers, a book, a ball, a folded newspaper, a lunch bag and binoculars. A recurring motif of Michel Goulet's work, the chair has always been "the pretext for meeting new people, sharing, communicating", as the artist explains. "It reveals what makes each of us unique, but also what brings us together, what positions us and what sharpens our awareness …"

HOSPITALLERS CONVENT GARDEN

Entrance via the Musée des Hospitalières de l'Hôtel-Dieu de Montréal at
201, avenue des Pins Ouest
• Guided tours a dozen times a year, on Sunday, 1:30 pm to 3:30 pm,
from May to September
• Reservation required: call 514 849 2919
• Métro: Sherbrooke

> *"The silence and harmony of this place aids the healing process"*

At the heart of the city, behind 201, avenue des Pins Ouest, lies the large, secret garden of the Hospitallers convent. Sister Denise Lafond, Mother Superior of the main convent of the Hospitallers of Saint Joseph, describes this special place as follows: "Our garden is meant to be a place of contemplation. The patients who visit it regularly find it to be a source of inner peace, and the silence and harmony of this place aids the healing process."

The garden of the Hospitallers is one of the last remaining green spaces of the so-called "Land of Providence" that once covered over 150 arpents (51 hectares).

The sons of Bénigne Basset, Montreal's first notary, gave this large property to the nuns in 1730. In exchange, the nuns housed and cared for them until their death. In addition to farming and stockraising, the nuns ran a quarry on the property and tended a garden dotted with numerous fruit trees.

When, in 1859, pollution and lack of space forced the Hôtel-Dieu Hospital out of Old Montreal, this Land of Providence was chosen as the site for a new convent and hospital. At the time, the area north of rue Sherbrooke was still undeveloped.

From then on, the garden was used to feed the religious community and its patients, supplying nearly all the fruit and vegetables the sisters and their patients needed, and the stables along the south-west garden wall housed twenty-eight dairy cows and several hundred chickens. So, the nuns supplied their own milk, cream and eggs until 1932. In addition to providing food, the garden also became a place for contemplation and meditation.

Today, the hospital's patients and the last nuns of the community continue to enjoy this green space. The animals are gone, but the fruit trees are still there and, in 2011, the nuns even installed new beehives to replace those removed in 1930.

You can still enjoy a bit of this countryside today by taking one of the guided tours given a dozen Sundays a year for a limited number of guests. This is also the perfect opportunity to discover a graceful yet tiny chapel dedicated to the Virgin concealed among the trees, as it's only open to visitors during the tours.

L'AMOUR CINEMA

4015, boulevard Saint-Laurent
• Tel: 514 849 6227
• Métro: Mont-Royal

A unique history

It's hard to believe the tantalizing façade of the L'Amour pornographic cinema hides a historic theatre worthy of being listed among Montreal's heritage sites.

The history of this building at the heart of The Main (boulevard Saint-Laurent) is quite unique. The current L'Amour cinema began its "career" as the "Globe" in 1914. Both theatre and cinema, like most venues of the time, the Globe took up residence in this rapidly growing Jewish neighbourhood of Montreal. In the 1920s and 1930s, films in Yiddish were shown here. When the theatre expanded its programming in 1932, it took on a new name, "Hollywood".

It wasn't until 1969 that the theatre specialized once again, this time in pornographic movies, and took on a new name: "Pussycat". It finally became the L'Amour theatre in 1981.

Miraculously, its interior has barely changed: the promenade gallery, horseshoe balcony and stage are still intact and close to their original condition. Although today the L'Amour is the oldest theatre of its kind in Montreal, it is probably also the last. Technical innovations such as the VCR, DVD players and the internet have put an end to the projection of sexual prowess on the big screen. The 1970s boom of pornographic movies is well behind us. At the time, people queued to get in, while today they enter on the sly.

Audiences are small, as new viewers are attracted more by a sense of voyeurism and exhibitionism than by the films themselves. That's why a section especially for couples was created about ten years ago.

The "Globe" of yesteryear hasn't taken its last breath yet, however. On some evenings, the theatre becomes a venue for alternative culture. Every year, concerts are given here as part of the "Pop Montréal" independent music festival, and on "Grindhouse Wednesdays" (the first Wednesday of every month), atypical "underground" films from the 1940s to 1970s are shown and accompanied by musical performances. The theatre thus continues to thumb its nose at conformity, as fits the site's mismatched decor.

BENCHES OF THE PORTUGUESE DISTRICT ❺

Boulevard Saint-Laurent on Plateau Mont-Royal
• Métro: Saint-Laurent or Mont-Royal

An original literary walk

Since April, 2009, twelve public benches in black granite have been installed along The Main between rue Saint-Cuthbert and rue Marie-Anne. The six benches on the east side, and six others on the west, seem to create a symbolic bridge. Each bench is engraved with a quotation in Portuguese and in French taken from major Portuguese authors of the 14th to 21st centuries. They range from the courtly songs of the troubadour king Dom Dinis and the works of Nobel Laureate José Saramago, to that most famous of Portuguese poets, Fernando Pessoa.

For each author, a brief biography and a short description of the literary and historic contexts of the work are provided in French and Portuguese. Theatre, religion, the great maritime discoveries, Portuguese Baroque, fado, travel, emigration and language are just some of the themes examined along this very original literary walk.

The sides of each bench are decorated with azulejos (painted ceramic tiles) designed by four Montreal artists of Portuguese origin: Carlos Calado, Miguel Rebelo, Joe Lima and Joseph Branco.

This was the city's way of commemorating the fifty-year presence of the Portuguese community in Montreal. It's a beautiful way to meander through the complexities of the Lusitanian culture and soul.

NEARBY
PARC DU PORTUGAL

Corner of rue Marie-Anne and boulevard Saint-Laurent

Portugal Park is a charming little spot that pays homage to Portuguese immigrants, most of whom came from the Azores and began settling here in the 1950s. The park is dotted with decorative elements relating to Portuguese culture, including a bandstand topped by a Cock of Barcelos and a fountain decorated with azulejos by Ruiz Dias.

The pedestal is a reminder of how explorers once marked their arrival in the new lands they discovered. Here, it symbolizes the presence of the Portuguese community.

RUE DEMERS ❻

• Métro: Laurier or Mont-Royal

Flowers in the roadway

This little street north of Plateau Mont-Royal, lined by houses built in the early 20th century for the workers of the nearby quarries, seems like any other back lane in the neighbourhood. However, rue Demers, wedged between avenues Coloniale and Henri-Julien and parallel to boulevard Saint-Joseph and rue Villeneuve, leads a double life.

Although one section is still open to traffic, the other has been turned into a garden.

The history of this lane is extraordinary. In 1969, five architecture students suggested renovating it, in association with the residents, to improve what was then a run-down neighbourhood. The young architects failed to complete their project, blocked by the residents' lack of enthusiasm and failure to participate. A film entitled *Les fleurs c'est pour Rosemont* (The Flowers are for Rosemont), which is still available on the ONF–NFB (National Film Board of Canada) website, recounts their adventure.

Forty years later, however, rue Demers has become one of the pleasantest spots of this part of Mile End and is considerably more middle class. The residents have finally succeeded in upgrading their surroundings by creating large green areas that actually block the roadway and by taking great care of the appearance of their homes. Enjoy a tranquil stroll along the street to take in its peace and quiet. Change of scenery guaranteed!

THE PLATEAU'S GREEN LANES

Back lanes are a distinctive – and even emblematic – feature of the city of Montreal. Indeed, few cities have such a network of them. Montreal's 4,000 or so are estimated to have a cumulative length of almost 450 kilometres! Over the past twenty years, these green lanes have grown up, first rapidly taking over the Plateau Mont-Royal neighbourhood before spreading to the rest of Montreal Island. There are more than fifty of them on the "Plateau" and a dozen are added every year.

For a street to become "green", around 70 square metres of the asphalt surface has to be removed and replaced by flower beds of perennials, trees and bushes. Increasing the amount of greenery helps to reduce the effects of urban heat, recuperates rainwater and increases biodiversity. It is also a way to fraternize with neighbours and beautify the district. The decision to create a green lane is always up to the residents, who form a committee. If 100% of them approve, the street can even be prohibited to traffic, thus becoming a proper garden. This is what is called a *ruelle champêtre* (country lane), the first of which was created in 2007, between avenue Drolet and avenue Henri-Julien.

MUSEUM OF THE AUXILIARY FIRE FIGHTERS ❼
OF MONTREAL

5100, boulevard Saint-Laurent in fire station No. 30
- Tel: 514 872 3757
- Guided tours on Sunday only, 1:30 pm to 4 pm
- Métro: Laurier

To the glory of firemen

T he small museum of the Auxiliary Fire Fighters of Montreal, at 5100, boulevard Saint-Laurent, is a bridge between the past and present. The modest but very well-documented exhibition rooms have been set up within fire station No. 30, which is still in operation. Furthermore, the guided tours are led by auxiliary firemen who love their profession and enjoy telling about its history. You thus learn that Montreal's development is closely related to its firefighters.

From the moment the city was founded in 1642, fire sometimes became a fiercer enemy than the Iroquois. The military and night watchmen defended the city against fire, as they patrolled the streets to watch out for danger and sound the alarm in the case of fire.

In the 17th and 18th centuries, numerous buildings went up in flames. In 1765 and 1767 respectively, fires destroyed 108 and 90 houses, leaving hundreds of families homeless. The Hôtel-Dieu Hospital was also destroyed several times. In the 19th century, firefighting became an organized affair. The first hand pumps appeared, as did the first "fire clubs" associated with insurance companies. In 1829, Montreal had three separate fire clubs: the Saint-Lawrence Alliance and Fire Club of Montreal, the Montreal Fire Club, and the Phoenix Volunteer Fire Club. Unfortunately, there was strong rivalry among the volunteers of these different clubs. The first to arrive on the scene claimed the exclusive right to fight the fire in the name of their club. These squabbles and skirmishes between firefighters often gave the blaze time to spread …

A permanent firefighting company wasn't organized until 1863. In 1911, the first motor vehicles progressively replaced the horse-drawn carts; the last horses were retired from service in 1936. The post-war era brought along its share of new techniques, better communication and improved training, thus leading to the Sécurité Incendie de Montréal (Montreal Fire Department) of today. Note, however, that Montreal didn't welcome its first female firefighter until 1990.

This entire firefighting adventure is recounted on the two floors of the museum on boulevard Saint-Laurent: machines from yesteryear, old photographs, a helmet collection, and more. The tour ends in the fire station in front of the famous red fire trucks with their gleaming chrome – an hour and a half of true pleasure.

WILENSKY'S LIGHT LUNCH ❽

34, avenue Fairmount Ouest (corner of Clark)
- Tel: 514 271 0247
- Métro: Laurier
- Monday to Saturday, 9 am to 4 pm, closed Sunday
- Cash only

> *"If we keep it this way long enough, it'll come back in fashion one day!"*

Y ou could often walk past this old, bright green façade without realizing it's a restaurant.

Canteen, delicatessen, take out ... Wilensky's Light Lunch is a mix of all that but, above all, it's a page out of the history of Montreal's Jewish neighbourhood, of which it is one of the last remaining "monuments".

It all began with a family that emigrated from Russia in the late 19th century. The grandfather, a barber, had a small shop where he also sold cigars. In 1932, in the middle of the Depression, the 20-year-old son Moe and his brother Archie decided to open their own business, a canteen restaurant where customers could also borrow books. It quickly became a meeting place for the Jewish community, even if the competition soon forced them to do something different.

The two brothers had the idea of buying a grill to make hot sandwiches, like the paninis you can find today. "Wilensky's Special" was born: a combination of salami and bologna sausage on a Kaiser roll spread with yellow mustard.

Today, entering the restaurant is like entering a museum: the simple decor seems timeless. It also perfectly corresponds to the description given by celebrated Montreal author Mordecai Richler, who immortalized the place in *The Apprenticeship of Duddy Kravitz*, a novel published in 1959 that was adapted for the screen in 1974: a nearly empty large room, a few old photos

and newspaper articles stuck on the wall, a wooden bookcase with some old books and, at the back, a "vintage" counter standing behind three rickety stools. The menu hasn't changed either: hot dogs, sliced egg sandwiches, or The Special (with or without cheese) accompanied by an old-fashioned flavoured soda from the fountain and, for dessert, a New York Egg Cream, a milk-based soda. For Sharon Wilensky, who runs the restaurant with her mother Ruth, Moe's wife, there's no need to change a formula that works, "In any case, if we keep it that way long enough, it'll come back in fashion one day!"

Moe with his brother Archie and a customer soon after the restaurant opened.

HEBREW TRACES AT MONTREAL'S COLLÈGE FRANÇAIS

⑨

Collège Français of Montreal
162, rue Fairmount-Ouest
• Métro: Laurier

Fragments of a former synagogue

I t is hard to image that the architecturally uninteresting and modern façade of the Collège Français actually conceals a former synagogue. From the late 19th to early 20th centuries, a large Eastern European Jewish population immigrated to Montreal. Nicknamed "America's little Jerusalem", Montreal was a capital of Jewish culture in America. In 1930, 60,000 people in the city spoke Yiddish and many synagogues were built, including the B'nai Jacob synagogue on rue Fairmount, in 1918.

When the community scattered to new neighbourhoods built after the Second World War, several synagogues in the former Jewish district were reconverted. The B'nai Jacob synagogue was sold to the Collège Français in the 1950s.

Most of the original building has survived, although its façade has been disfigured by a brick extension housing new flights of steps. Strangely, you can still see a part of the old arch that once protected a rose window depicting the Star of David. A few letters in Hebrew are also still visible. At ground level, the large fresco on each side of the entrance includes a flaming sun, perhaps a reminder of the large Jewish star that once graced the façade.

GLEN LE MESURIER'S "TWILIGHT SCULPTURE GARDEN"

10

Corner of avenue Van-Horne and rue Saint-Urbain, near Saint-Laurent viaduct
• Métro: Rosemount

> *When art colonizes an empty lot*

Glen Le Mesurier is one of those passionate artists whose approach goes far beyond the artworks themselves. He is a vehement supporter of public art who yearns to see cities filled with works of art. In 1999, he set his sights on an empty lot near his Mile End studio and decided to turn it into a sculpture garden. This abandoned lot, covered with debris of all sorts and contaminated by gas from the Irving gas station that once stood there, was transformed in 1999, becoming a green park dotted with about fifty works created from recycled metal, most of which came from the old Outremont marshalling yard. With help from a horticulturist, Glen established a list of plants and bushes that could help to purify the soil: raspberries, wildflowers, mint …

Near the tracks, he set up a beehive to encourage the pollination of all this new greenery. Then he started installing his sculptures, at no cost and surreptitiously – most often at the end of the day when no one was paying attention, hence the name "Twilight sculpture garden". Some works stand more than 5 metres tall and can't be missed: animals and plants, strange weather vanes turning with the wind, and towers of wheels and gears. The city authorities, concerned about his illicit occupation of space, first threatened to demolish the artworks, but sense prevailed after a while and his original project was accepted. Today the authorities have even recognized the artist's moral ownership of the lot. Defining himself as a "green" artist, Glen Le Mesurier continues to create public art to this day. Some of his works are held in private collections, of course, but most of them are exhibited in places accessible to a wide audience, such as Douglas Hospital (see page 183) or, more recently, square Cabot.

CAO DAI TEMPLE OF MONTREAL

7161, rue Saint-Urbain
- Tel: 514 277 5450
- Métro: De-Castelnau
- Open primarily during Sunday morning services from 11:30 am

A converted synagogue

The beautiful yellow house at 7161, rue Saint-Urbain, between rue Jean-Talon Ouest and avenue Mozart, stands out in this rather grey district of industrial warehouses.

Since 1992, it has been the home of the Cao Dai Temple of Montreal, although its history goes back much further.

The place was first a synagogue, built in 1910 in this working-class neighbourhood largely populated by Italian immigrants. A small Jewish minority lived here and they baptized their synagogue Poelei Zedek (meaning "workers for justice"). Indeed, many of its members were carpenters and labourers who worked at the large rail complex nearby.

After the end of the Second World War, the synagogue gradually lost its congregation as they left the neighbourhood for the west side of the island. It was forced to close after a fire in 1988, and risked being demolished completely.

The building was finally saved and sold to the Vietnamese Cao Dai community (see below), which opened its temple in 1992. Inside, the cosy decor of woodwork and curtains plays backdrop to a light-filled and colourful atmosphere where cushions have replaced the pews. Visitors are welcome to attend the Sunday morning services. Caodaiists are more than happy to share their traditions.

WHAT IS CAO DAI?

In Vietnamese, Cao Dai means "High Tower" or "Raised Palace". It is also a symbolic name referring to God the Father, the supreme being.

Established in 1921 in Vietnam's Tay Ninh province, Cao Dai is a religion that follows much of the teachings of Buddhism.

Today, it has roughly five million followers worldwide. Caodaiists worship God, represented by the Divine Eye, but also Shakyamuni Buddha, Laozi and Confucius. They also venerate great historical figures such as Victor Hugo, Joan of Arc, Louis Pasteur, Churchill, Lenin and Shakespeare.

PORTRAIT OF MUSSOLINI

Madonna della Difesa church
6800, rue Henri-Julien, corner of rue Dante in Little Italy
• Métro: Jean-Talon or Beaubien

Il Duce
on horseback
in church

A rtist Guido Nincheri decorated many churches from Boston to Vancouver, including the Madonna della Difesa in Montreal's Little Italy, north of boulevard Saint-Laurent. Among the angels and saints you'll find an unexpected figure: Il Duce, Benito Mussolini.

The history of this fresco is closely linked to that of the Italian immigration to Montreal. From 1901 to 1911, the number of Italian immigrants grew from 1,630 to 7,013.

In 1910, these new, strongly religious immigrants created the Madonna della Difesa parish, inaugurating the church of the same name in 1919.

Beginning in 1925, the Italian Consul, under the supervision of fascist Italy, planned propaganda operations in order to increase Mussolini's popularity among the Italian community in North America. The authoritarian regime wanted to gain followers in Canada and intensify their patriotism.

It was in this context that some of the frescoes in Madonna della Difesa were painted. Completed from 1930 to 1933 by Guido Nincheri, the apse depicts a rather usual scene, to say the least, in relation to the current events of the time. Above, you can see Pope Pius XI and his retinue and, below, Mussolini in ceremonial regalia astride a horse. What lies behind this fresco, which is so shocking today? In fact, the painting honours the Lateran Treaty, made in 1929 between the Holy See and the Italian government, then represented by Mussolini. This treaty led to the recognition of the State of the Vatican City.

When Italy entered the war, in 1940, thousands of Italians suspected of being sympathizers of Mussolini's regime were interned in military camps all over the Canadian territory. Among them was artist Guido Nincheri, who was accused of being a fascist sympathizer because of his Mussolini portrait in the church. He was only kept in detention for three months because his wife managed to secure his release. She demonstrated that the church leaders had requested the portrait of the dictator and that her husband was obliged to paint it, for fear of losing the commission. After receiving complaints regarding the impropriety of having an image of the dictator in a place of worship, Mussolini and his soldiers were hidden behind sheets of paper for seven years, until September, 1947. The officials of the time decided to accept this testimony to a dark period of Italian history and to conserve the fresco as visitors of this neighbourhood church can still see it today.

MUSSOLINI SYMBOLS OF CASA D'ITALIA

505, rue Jean-Talon Est (corner of rue Berri)
• Tel: 514 271 2524
• Métro: Jean-Talon, Berri exit

A turbulent past

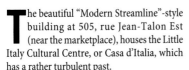

The beautiful "Modern Streamline"-style building at 505, rue Jean-Talon Est (near the marketplace), houses the Little Italy Cultural Centre, or Casa d'Italia, which has a rather turbulent past.

Built in 1936 by architect Patsy (Pasquale) Colangelo, the Casa d'Italia was, for many years, the central gathering place for immigrants arriving from Italy. Its architecture, one of the last expressions of the Art Deco movement, accentuates curved shapes highlighted by long, horizontal lines, and sometimes incorporates elements borrowed from the maritime industry, such as railings and portholes.

At the time, around fifty cities had their own Casa d'Italia, yet Montreal is one of the few where the building is still used for its original purpose. And this is no mean feat. During the Second World War, the building was sequestered before being occupied by the Canadian Army, who suspected its members of maintaining ties with Mussolini's Fascist regime. The famous fasces of the dictatorial Italian regime can be found in the sculptures on the outside walls and on the terrazzo flooring of the second floor.

Finally, the centre reopened in January, 1947, but its troubles weren't over. Twenty years later, it was almost demolished to make way for the nearby Jean-Talon métro station.

The building was clearly meant to last. In 2009, it was completely restored and enlarged during an extensive conversion into a place of memory for the Italian community and an ecomuseum of immigration and integration into Quebec society, thereby reviving its spirit.

MONT-ROYAL, OUTREMONT, WESTMOUNT, NDG

MONT-ROYAL'S HIDDEN VIEWPOINT

Uphill access: take the path that begins at avenue des Pins and Redpath Crescent just west of rue Peel
Downhill access: opposite the city, left of the chalet at Kondiaronk Lookout

*For
your eyes
only*

You can't visit Montreal without seeing Mont-Royal. It's visible from every direction, from the elegant neighbourhoods of Westmount and Outremont, to the streets of the Plateau Mont-Royal district and the downtown skyscrapers.

Beloved by Montreal's residents, it's more than just a hill – it's the symbol of a city and a population protected from urban development. Yet the residents and tourists who have had the time and inclination to discover all of Mont-Royal are few and far between. Most visitors just climb to the top and stop off at the Voie Camillien-Houde car park before going to the Kondiaronk Lookout. They've seen Beaver Lake (Lac des Castors) and its winter ice-skating rink, but few have wandered along this mini-mountain's numerous paths, which sometimes offer pleasant surprises. That's the type of hike we'd suggest. As you leave the park's chalet, a narrow path heads eastward along the steep slope and, a few hundred metres later, leads to a small natural viewpoint equipped with a simple metal barrier to keep visitors from falling. The view from here is essentially the same as that from the Kondiaronk, but it's much more romantic as you'll probably be the only ones around. Getting here is rather more difficult in winter, but the scenery is even more beautiful. For the more athletic, you can also reach this little promontory by climbing the 256 steps of the giant wooden stairway that starts at avenue des Pins near rue Peel.

THE SAME LANDSCAPER AS NEW YORK'S CENTRAL PARK
Inaugurated on May 24, 1876, Queen Victoria's birthday, Parc du Mont-Royal was the work of Frederick Law Olmsted, who had previously designed New York's famous Central Park.

THE HIGHEST POINT OF THE CITY

The observatory at the top of Saint Joseph's Oratory, which offers a view of the entire city, is the highest point on Montreal Island at 263 metres.

THE EIFFEL TOWER BELLS

In the Oratory, the fifty-six bronze bells made by Paccard et Frères foundry were originally destined for the Eiffel Tower in Paris.

THE FORGOTTEN STORY OF THE MONT-ROYAL ILLUMINATED CROSS

Christmas, 1642. Fort Ville-Marie, built in the spring, risks being flooded. High waters threaten to demolish the fragile construction, which cannot resist the waters of the Saint Lawrence River.

Paul de Chomedey, sieur (lord) of Maisonneuve, prays to the Holy Virgin to spare his new colony and vows to plant a cross at the top of Mont-Royal if his prayer is answered. Such is the case and, on January 6, 1643, the day of Epiphany, the governor of Montreal himself carries the promised cross up the hill and plants it at the summit. A stained-glass window in Notre-Dame church illustrates this epic ascension of Mont-Royal.

In 1874, to celebrate its 40th anniversary, the Saint John the Baptist Society proposed to erect a new cross in memory of the Maisonneuve cross. It took another fifty years before the project came to completion. To raise the funds, 104,200 volunteers (4,200 adults and 100,000 students in Quebec) sold stamps picturing the Mont-Royal cross. $10,000 was raised by the sale of these 5 cent stamps. Construction began on May 16, 1924.

On December 24 of the same year, the cross illuminated the skies of Montreal for the first time. In 2009, extensive renovation work gave it a new lease of life.

OTHER LITTLE-KNOWN FACTS ABOUT THE ILLUMINATED CROSS

The 31 metre cross towers at a height of 252 metres and is visible 80 kilometres away.

Its steel structure weighs 26 tonnes.

The colour of the light bulbs changes for special events. Generally white, they become purple at the death of a pope or king. The colour yellow indicates a coronation.

Facing eastward, the cross marks the symbolic appropriation of the city by the francophone population.

In 1988, Hans Marotte, a student and Quebec separatist, climbed the cross to hang a huge flag in support of Bill 101,* earning himself instant notoriety throughout the country.

---

*The 1977 Charter of the French Language (La Charte de la langue française), also known as Bill 101 (Loi 101), defines French as the official language of Quebec.

CIMETIÈRE MONT-ROYAL ARBORETUM ❸

Entrance: 1297, chemin de la Forêt, Outremont (at the end of the
extension road of boulevard du Mont-Royal which continues avenue du
Mont-Royal)
• Tel: 514 279 7358
• Métro: Édouard-Montpetit

The essence of nature

I n Montreal, everyone is familiar with the two large cemeteries spread across the slopes of the mount, Notre-Dame-des-Neiges and Mont-Royal. Few, however, know that Mont-Royal cemetery is also home to an arboretum containing more than 100 tree species that provide shelter for 145 different species of bird.

Construction of the cemetery began in 1852. At the time, the city's various burial grounds were reaching maximum capacity and new ones were needed. Following the designs of American landscapers James Sidney and James P.W. Neff, this new site was created in the Romantic style of 19th-century "rural" cemeteries.

Mont-Royal cemetery is composed of a succession of terraces which follow the natural contours of the slopes. You can stroll through its 66 hectares (165 acres) as you would a large garden. At the entrance at 1297, chemin de la Fôret, ask for the map that indicates the positions of the various deciduous and conifer trees. For each tree indicated, an informative plaque provides its common and Latin names. Guided tours led by naturalists are also organized, especially in spring and autumn when the park reveals all its beauty.

Every year, new trees and bushes are planted, increasing the arboretum's

richness. Such diversity naturally attracts a large variety of birds and many migrating species stop here in spring and summer. Tree swallows and bluebirds nest in the birdhouses installed by park staff. Among the species that nest in the cemetery you'll find the screech owl, blue jay, American robin, tits, mockingbirds, and more.

In addition to the panoramic view, the top of the mount is the ideal spot to observe the flight of the falcons. You'd almost forget that more than 200,000 people are buried here.

SAINT JOHN THE BAPTIST WOODS ❹

The Saint John the Baptist Woods path begins at the far west end
of boulevard Mont-Royal (at No. 1344) where it becomes avenue
Courcelette
• A 1.5 kilometre round-trip hike
• Métro: Édouard-Montpetit

> *The overlooked section of Mont-Royal*

Saint John the Baptist Woods, located
on the northern slopes of Mont-Royal,
is named for the funeral processions
that in the 19th century often passed through
these woods from Saint John the Baptist
parish to Notre-Dame-des-Neiges cemetery.

Starting in the hills of the up-market
Outremont neighbourhood, the path quietly winds its way to one of the peaks,
reaching an altitude of 211 metres. Unfortunately, the view from the peak
is hidden by the trees. However, a promontory overlooking the University
of Montreal offers an impressive panorama of northern Montreal and the
surrounding area up to the foothills of the Laurentians. Notre-Dame-des-
Neiges cemetery, the owner and guardian of this little woodland of around
10 hectares, has constantly protected it from numerous development projects.
Rich in biodiversity and renowned for their oak trees, the Saint John the
Baptist Woods are home to a ramp (wild leek) colony, probably the last
remaining on Mont-Royal.

Although open to the public, this part of the mount is often overlooked.
The only visitors are well-informed hikers and keen mountain bikers. Soon,
a new park will be opened on this northern slope which will include the Saint
John the Baptist Woods as well as those of the University of Montreal. Adding
to Mont-Royal Park, dating from 1876, and Summit Park, created on the
western slope in 1940, the "Third Summit" park will cover 23 hectares.

Once the works are finished, the park will be a major component of the
ring-road around the mount, which will include a 10 kilometre loop for hiking
and biking. In the meantime, you can still enjoy the privacy of Saint John the
Baptist Woods and their well-kept secret.

NEARBY

AVENUE MAPLEWOOD
Nicknamed the "avenue of power" because of the several influential
Quebeckers that have lived or still live in these opulent homes on Outremont
hill, avenue Maplewood is the site of some beautiful residences, such as the
semi-detached homes at Nos. 47 and 49 dating from 1906, the oldest on
the street. Also of note are the Corbeil House at No. 41, a small château
reminiscent of French Renaissance manors, and the beautiful American
colonial-style home at No. 77. Between avenues Springgrove and Pagnuelo,
don't miss Sévère Godin's colossal residence (No. 153), the English-inspired
homes at Nos. 159 and 161, and finally the modern residence of former
Quebec Premier Robert Bourassa at No. 190.

SAINT-ALBERT-LE-GRAND MONASTERY   ❺

2715, chemin de la Côte-Sainte-Catherine
• Métro: Université-de-Montréal

A rare example of modern architecture in Quebec

The tall silhouette of its openwork tower catches the eye of drivers along chemin de la Côte-Sainte-Catherine. As you approach, two large green crosses reveal the function of this religious monument. Saint-Albert-le-Grand monastery, the work of Quebec architect Yves Bélanger, is undoubtedly his most remarkable achievement.

The monastic complex, inaugurated in 1960 during a period of revival of religious architecture, is a rare example of modern architecture in Quebec. It is composed of three main volumes placed in a triangle around a cloister. The chapel and its steeple face chemin de la Côte-Sainte-Catherine and the novitiate borders the street, while the private wing of the monastery unites the two former volumes diagonally.

The complex is built of exposed blocks of rough concrete and yellow brick, and the simplicity of its decoration allows for greater play of light. Inside the church, the geometric shapes and squares of coloured glass break up the light in unexpected ways.

In 1954, when the Dominican fathers purchased a plot of land from the Montreal Hunt, an English fox-hunting club, the idea was to build their monastery near the intellectual elite of the nearby University of Montreal, and thus follow their secular tradition of spreading faith and knowledge. At its inauguration, the monastery served as a place of instruction for boarding students and was home to about a hundred monks. Today, Dominican fathers still live in part of the complex, while the rest has been subdivided and let out, notably to the International Bureau for Children's Rights.

Albrecht von Bollstädt, known as Saint Albertus Magnus or Albert the Great (1193–1280), was a German friar, philosopher, naturalist and alchemist of the Middle Ages. A renowned professor, he taught countless students in several cities, including Saint Thomas Aquinas in Paris. After joining the Dominican Order in Padua in 1223, he spent his life travelling around Europe and died at the ripe old age of 87. He was not canonized until 1931, however, by Pope Pius XI.

EUDORE DUBEAU MUSEUM OF DENTISTRY

University of Montreal Faculty of Dentistry
Pavillon Roger-Gaudry – Entrance B-1
2900, boulevard Édouard-Montpetit
• Visits by appointment: call 514 343 6111, ext. 2877
• Admission free
• Métro: Université-de-Montréal

*A dental
curiosity
cabinet*

T he Eudore Dubeau Museum of Dentistry is probably the most incongruous museum in Montreal, but also one of the most entertaining and interesting. It is hidden away in the University of Montreal's Faculty of Dentistry.

Due to a lack of means, there are no set opening hours, but the museum's director, Dr Denys Ruel, or one of his assistants will be more than happy to take you on a guided tour.

Exploring this little space filled with nearly 3,000 objects is a fascinating experience. Visitors are instantly drawn into the world of dentistry by a magnificent tooth-puller's chair, the same type used until the 1950s by pseudo-dentists who plied their trade outdoors, in front of the church on Sunday. At the time, it cost 25 cents to have a tooth removed … with no anaesthetic!

Next, you come across a mixed collection of instruments, spittoons and other anaesthesia and X-ray equipment, some of which make you shiver. Countless engravings, photos and drawings retrace the progress of the dental profession over the decades. Lined up in one of the display cases is a selection of skulls that came from the university's centre for the study of human growth, which closed in 1986. The skulls were rescued by a caretaker who

found them in the bin.

One of the highlights of the museum's collection, according to Dr Ruel, is a two-volume copy of Pierre Fauchard's *The Surgeon Dentist, or Treatise on the Teeth*, published in 1728, because there are only eleven known copies left in the world.

The curious and enthusiastic mustn't miss this curiosity cabinet dedicated to the world of dentistry, which pays tribute to Dr Eudore Dubeau, who founded the Montreal school of dental surgery in 1904.

THE ORATORY'S SECRET GARDEN

Oratoire Saint-Joseph-du-Mont-Royal
3800, chemin Queen-Mary
• Tel: 514 733 8211
• Métro: Côte-des-Neiges

*Calm above
the city hubbub*

ew Montreal residents have ever stepped into the city's best-known religious building, and even fewer have visited the adjoining gardens, known as the *Chemin de Croix* (Way of the Cross). You reach the gardens via a path that begins halfway up the hill of Saint Joseph's Oratory, at 3800, chemin Queen Mary.

An auspicious spot for contemplation and meditation, this magnificent garden was designed by Frederick G. Todd, who also designed the layout of Mont-Royal and the Plains of Abraham Park in Quebec. The seventeen sculptures that embellish this full-scale *Chemin de Croix* were created in plaster by Montreal sculptor Louis Parent, who dedicated ten years of his life to them (1943–1953). They were then sculpted in natural Indiana limestone and Carrara marble from Italy by Ercolo Barbieri.

Inaugurated in 1951, fourteen years after Brother André's death, this garden brought to life the holy man's dream of offering pilgrims a special place for prayer and meditation imbued with the mystery of Christ's Passion. Today, believers and non-believers alike can enjoy the tranquility of this unique site that winds along the hillside above the city hubbub.

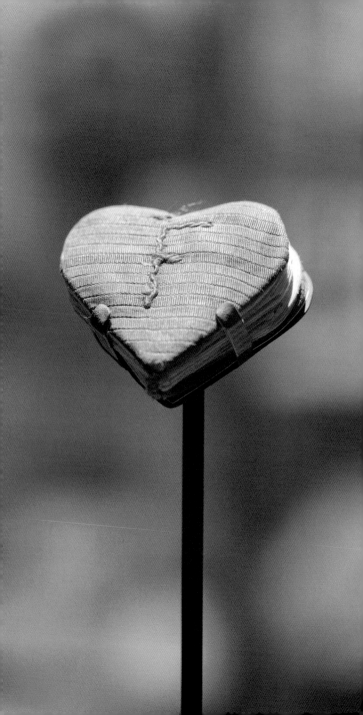

THE HEART OF AUSCHWITZ ❽

Montreal Holocaust Memorial Centre
5151, chemin de la Côte-Sainte-Catherine
• Métro: Côte-Sainte-Catherine or Snowdon
• Open Sunday to Friday
• $8 for adults, $5 for students and those over 65
• Tel: 514 345 2605 • www.mhmc.ca

"Freedom, Freedom, Freedom"

This is the story of a tiny heart that beats within a site dedicated to the memory of the Jewish Holocaust of the Second World War. Barely bigger than a pebble, and heart-shaped, it looks like a little book whose cover is embroidered with the letter F. The inside unfolds like an origami, revealing a dozen pages.

It's December 12, 1944, and Fania Feiner (née Landau) is celebrating her twentieth birthday. She is also a prisoner at Auschwitz, in Poland. In the munitions factory where she works, her friend Zlatka Pitluk (née Schneiderhaus) wants to give her a present. In this life in captivity where nothing is accessible, she shows her ingenuity and perseverance to find the paper, fabric and tools she needs to make this little heart, which she has signed by almost all the twenty or so women who work with her and Fania. They write messages of friendship and hope in their respective languages: Polish, German, French and Hebrew. Among the messages, one reads: "With others, laugh. When you cry, hide", and "Our victory will be not dying". And Fania's favourite, "Freedom, Freedom, Freedom".

At great personal risk and by using every possible subterfuge, Fania kept the little heart under her arm throughout the rest of her detention and during the terrible "death march" from Auschwitz to Ravensbruck. Those who survived were finally liberated in April, 1945.

After having treasured it for more than half a century, Fania Feiner donated the heart to the Montreal Centre, where it lies today. In the midst of hell, these courageous women committed an act of humanity, the strength of which has survived to inspire us today.

NEARBY

SPANISH AND PORTUGUESE SYNAGOGUE (SHEARITH ISRAEL)
4894, avenue Saint-Kevin

The Spanish and Portuguese synagogue, the city's first synagogue in 1768, is one of the most beautiful in Montreal. First located in Old Montreal between rue Notre-Dame and rue Saint-Jacques, it was moved four times over the centuries before settling at its current site in the Snowdon neighbourhood in 1947.

ROYAL VICTORIA HOSPITAL SWIMMING POOL ❾

In the hospital grounds
687, avenue des Pins Ouest
• Métro: McGill ou Peel
• Admission: $5

A well-kept secret

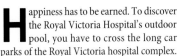appiness has to be earned. To discover the Royal Victoria Hospital's outdoor pool, you have to cross the long car parks of the Royal Victoria hospital complex. Climb a dozen rather dilapidated steps and you'll find yourself in an oasis of greenery, with Mont-Royal Park on one side and a magnificent view of the city and its skyscrapers on the other. This site is the well-kept secret of those who enjoy a tranquil dip.

Although the employees of the hospital and nearby McGill University officially have priority here, the pool is open to the public "when there's room", for a $5 entry fee. The day we visited, on a beautiful August afternoon, there were only a few people happily enjoying this almost private pool.

THREE MORE OUTDOOR POOLS

Montreal is the North American city with the most outdoor pools. There are seventy-four of them, that's one pool for every 22,500 residents. Apart from the discreet Royal Victoria pool, here are three others that are less secluded but a joy to discover.

Île Sainte-Hélène Aquatic Complex, at the heart of Jean-Drapeau Park. Tel: 514 872 2323 www.parcjeandrapeau.com
Here you'll find a competition pool, a diving pool and a recreational pool. Every Saturday, children can play with huge inflatable structures that stand as high as 15 metres. $3 for children 3 to 13, $6 for adults, and $15 for families.

Pointe-Claire village pool, Bourgeau Park, 5, avenue Sainte-Anne, Pointe-Claire. Tel: 514 694 5966
Located in a large park where you can take part in several sports, this pool offers a view of the pretty Saint-Louis Lake marina. $3 for children, $5 for adults and $15 for families.

Verdun Natatorium, 6500, boulevard LaSalle. Tel: 514 765 7230
An Art Deco building inaugurated in July 1940, for several years the Natatorium was not only believed to be the largest outdoor public pool in Quebec, but also the largest in Canada. It can welcome up to 1,150 swimmers and, in 2005, a heated paddling pool with a maximum occupancy of 250 children was added to the complex. Children (age 6 to 17) $1; adults $2; children 5 and under free.

THE HORSE'S HEAD OF RAVENSCRAG HOUSE ⑩

Royal Victoria Hospital
1025, avenue des Pins Ouest (corner of rue McTavish)
• Métro: McGill

> **A former location for covert and illegal CIA research**

I n the mid-19th century, the hill of Mont-Royal was surrounded by pastures, orchards and large bourgeois homes belonging to wealthy families. Among them was Sir Hugh Allan, a prosperous businessman who made his fortune in shipping, banking and the burgeoning telephone industry. From 1861 to 1863, he entrusted architects Victor Roy and John Hopkins with the construction of a sumptuous residence in this luxurious neighbourhood that came to be known as the "Golden Square Mile". He named his home Ravenscrag in reference to a Scottish castle (Ravenscraig) that greatly impressed him during his travels.

Built in a style combining Italian Renaissance, neoclassicism and medieval Scottish architecture, this residence has had a unique destiny. From the beginning, its originality set it apart: its thirty-four rooms were each decorated in a different style. Its asymmetrical façade topped by an imposing rectangular tower looked down on the city from the heights of rue McTavish. The Allan family, great horse-lovers, also had one of the neighbourhood's most beautiful stables built on the home's 5.6 hectare (14 acre) property, the entrance to which is still there with its horse's head carved in stone.

In 1940, Sir Hugh Allan's heirs donated Ravenscrag to the Royal Victoria Hospital, and in 1943 it was renamed the Allan Memorial Institute of Psychiatry. The residence then went through a dire period. From 1956 to 1963, under the direction of Dr Ewen Cameron, the psychiatric establishment served as an experimental centre for a secret and illegal research programme for the CIA, under the code name MK-Ultra. This research, akin to that conducted by Dr Mengele, aimed to control people's minds and behaviour. Mentally ill patients were brainwashed, notably by injecting them with psychotropic substances such as LSD or subjecting them to massive electric shock treatments.

REDPATH CRESCENT

⓫

• Métro: Peel

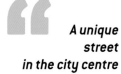

A unique street in the city centre

Located north of avenue des Pins on the southern slopes of Mont-Royal, between rue Drummond and rue de la Montagne, Redpath Crescent is a curved cul-de-sac lined with opulent homes, some of which are like miniature castles.

The nearby park that borders some of the properties adds to the prestige of this hidden section of the Golden Square Mile. More recent than most of the buildings of this famous bourgeois anglophone neighbourhood of Montreal, the construction of which began in 1850, the mansions on Redpath Crescent were built from the late 1910s to the early 1930s. A few more modern

residences were added in the 1960s and 1970s, but, as a whole, the luxurious nature of the architecture here is what gives the street its unique character. The less expensive "modest" homes are worth more than a million dollars, while the more beautiful properties with extensive lawns and unrestricted views of the city easily reach a value of five million dollars.

Among the must-see mansions are:

• **No. 1245**, the William Robert Grattan Holt House, built in 1927
• **No. 1260**, the Herbert Meredith Marler House (1915)
• **No. 1296**, the Ross Huntington McMaster House (1929)
• Right next door, at **No. 1297**, British diplomat James Richard Cross was kidnapped by armed men from the Front de Libération du Québec (Quebec Liberation Front) on October 5, 1970, thus plunging the country into crisis.
• **No. 1328**, the Francis Stuart Molson House, of the famous Molson brewery family (1930), is probably one of the street's most impressive mansions.
• **No. 1410**, the John R. McDougall House, dates from 1928. Its architect, A.T. Galt Durnford, won an architectural prize for the construction.

HIGH-RELIEF OF THE CORMIER HOUSE MUSE ⑫

1418, avenue des Pins Ouest
• Métro: Peel or Guy-Concordia

> **Two original homes on avenue des Pins**

The Cormier House was designed in 1930 by architect Ernest Cormier as his private home. A veritable architectural laboratory, the building illustrates a different style on three sides: Art Deco on the façade, monumental to the east, and modernist on the back. The architect also designed most of the furniture in the house, the other pieces being acquired at the 1925 International Exposition of Modern Industrial and Decorative Arts in Paris. The use of reinforced concrete in a residential building was very innovative for the period.

The residence, built on steeply sloping land, has one floor at the front, but four at the back. Also note the high-relief on the façade, depicting a muse supporting the central tower of the University of Montreal, the masterpiece of the architect who lived in this house until 1975. Afterwards, it was owned by Montreal designer Denis Robert. In 1980, it became the residence of Pierre Elliott Trudeau, Canadian Prime Minister. This famous politician lived here until his death in 2000. Indeed, many Montreal residents now call it the Trudeau House.

The Quebec government declared the house a historic monument in 1974.

NEARBY

CLARENCE DE SOLA HOUSE
1374, avenue des Pins Ouest

The Clarence de Sola House was built in 1913 for the son of Alexander Abraham de Sola, a rabbi and professor at McGill University. His son was a successful businessman and even served as the Belgian Consul in Montreal. In homage to the family's Spanish origins, this large bourgeois residence is inspired by Moorish architecture, notably the roof, entrance gate and the arched windows of its façade. As the house is built on the slope of the hill, it has the unusual characteristic of eight floors on the south side (opposite avenue du Musée) but only four on the side facing avenue des Pins.

The history of avenue des Pins is interesting. From 1859 to 1861, the Religious Hospitallers moved the Hôtel-Dieu hospital from Old Montreal to rue Saint-Urbain, where it still stands today. Three years later, in 1864, they granted the city the rights to a private road that ran alongside the hospital, then known as rue de l'Hôtel-Dieu. In 1875, Frederick Law Olmsted, who was in charge of designing Mont-Royal Park, planned a ring road at the base of the mount. Three streets were opened and named after trees, in English, as was common at the time: Elm, Cedar and Pine. Rue de l'Hôtel-Dieu became part of Pine Street; its name was officially translated into French in 1961, becoming rue des Pins. Today, avenue des Pins begins at rue Saint-Denis and still runs around a large part of the southern slopes of Mont-Royal.

VICIT LEO

SAINT LEO'S LIONS

Église Saint-Léon
4311, boulevard de Maisonneuve-Ouest
Corner of rue Clarke
• Tel: 514 935 4950
• Métro: Atwater
• Guided tours of the church and its masterpieces on the first and third
Mondays of each month at 1 pm

*Florentine
inspiration*

Not many Montreal residents are aware of Saint-Léon's church at 4311, boulevard de Maisonneuve-Ouest. Yet its varied interior decor surpasses everything to be found in Montreal's other churches.

It was the first Roman Catholic church to serve the francophone community in Westmount. Although there's nothing exceptional about its neo-Roman façade, its sobriety, beautiful proportions and powerful campanile are nevertheless striking. Those who are curious enough to climb the stairs will be well rewarded for the effort. Indeed, the interior conceals a decor so sumptuous it will take your breath away.

Once you've passed the shadowy narthex lit only by the lateral stained-glass windows, you enter the nave and can't help but gaze in wonder. In 1928, the parish priest Gauthier entrusted all the decoration to a popular artist of the period, Guido Nincheri, who made this church his masterpiece. He designed the interior plan, painted the murals and made the stained-glass windows. He also drew the designs of all the other ornamental elements for the cabinetwork, wood sculptures, altar, furniture, mosaics, and the bronze and marble works. He was assisted by many fellow Italian artists in this huge project, which took nearly thirty years to complete, from 1928 to 1957.

You mustn't miss the Florentine marble mosaics in the two wings of the transept. Using the "*pietra dura*" (hard stone) technique, the artist plays with nuances of colour and the veins in the marble to copy the original design as closely as possible. The two lions are a reference to Saint Leo I; the doves of peace, the wheat and the grapes, all products of the nourishing earth, thus nearly appear to be in relief.

Look up to discover the sharp, bright colours of the frescoes, which Nincheri created with the ancient technique of "*buon fresco*", or painting on wet plaster. The painter applies pure pigments, diluted in water, directly on the freshly whitewashed surface. The colours combine with the surface and become insoluble once dry, which requires the artist to act quickly.

WESTMOUNT BOWLING GREEN

401, avenue Kensington, corner of Sherbrooke
• Tel: 514 989 5532
• Annual subscription: $50 to $200

So Scottish!

Hardly any street noise, no music, a pristine silence barely broken by clinking balls and the whispered strategies of bowlers playing on a lawn so green you'd think it was artificial …

Westmount bowling green is a trip back in time. James Brown, a Scottish immigrant, introduced the world-renowned sport of lawn bowling to Quebec in 1902. He had already founded the Scottish Lawn Bowling Association in his home country twenty-eight years earlier. The Westmount Club was Quebec's first.

In 1903, it had only twenty-three members. Today there are seventy, most of whom are between the ages of 50 and 70.

This game, related to the French game *pétanque*, is played with a jack, not a *cochonnet*, and also uses different balls. The balls, called bowls, are not spherical, but slightly flattened at each end. Their shape is also asymmetrical because one of the ends is flatter than the other. This gives them an elliptical trajectory, which is particularly obvious when they roll slowly. To reach the target, the players must adjust the force and the line of trajectory. Each bowl weighs about 1.5 kilos.

Although bowling was once a sport reserved for the British aristocracy, the Westmount green has always been open to everyone, even though the club remained predominantly male for many years. Women were only allowed on Saturday afternoons … to serve tea.

They weren't accepted into the club until 1935, and it took another five years before mixed teams were allowed.

The current clubhouse and lawn are in fact almost identical replicas of the originals. Indeed, after being completely destroyed in 1996 to allow for the installation of an underground electricity sub-station, the club was rebuilt the following year.

WESTMOUNT'S VICTORIAN GREENHOUSES

4574, rue Sherbrooke Ouest
• Open Monday to Friday, 10 am to 9 pm (after 3 pm, entrance via the library), weekends and holidays, 10 am to 5 pm
• Admission free
• Métro: Atwater or Vendôme

Tranquil sensuality

Set between the municipal library and Victoria Hall, the greenhouses of Westmount Conservatory are timeless, a true haven of tranquility with an atmosphere conducive to meditation.

Also called the "Palm Tree House", this real little architectural gem, built in 1927 in the massive style of 19th-century British greenhouses, seems to defy gravity. Delicately set on a brick base, its ethereal double roof of steel and glass is one of the last two of that kind in Canada. Its feminine Moor-inspired curves are the work of the famous manufacturers Lord & Burnham, who are also credited with the greenhouses of the New York Botanical Garden and the United States Botanical Garden in Washington, D.C.

Over the years, the "Palm Tree House" has undergone various restorations. A vestibule was added and a pond was built in the main greenhouse.

In 2004, Westmount town hall undertook a programme of extensive work in which the upper glass and metal section of the greenhouse was taken down and restored before reassembly. Corroded steel and fractured cast-iron elements were replaced, as were any rotten wooden windows.

The pool in the main greenhouse was supplanted by a contemporary water basin with a small wooden bridge and Italian marble waterfall. Finally, a bronze fountain statue was installed to replace the one stolen in 1994.

You can enter the greenhouse through the library, handy when you need a study break and quite pleasant in winter when it's cold and the ground is covered in snow.

FORMER EMPRESS THEATRE

5560, rue Sherbrooke Ouest
• Métro: Vendôme

> *The only Egyptian-style palace built in Canada*

I t all began in 1927. Egypt and its mysteries were at the height of their popularity following the discovery of Tutankhamen's tomb a few years earlier. This new theatre in the Notre-Dame-de-Grâce (NDG) neighbourhood was built in the Art Deco style of the period, but with a slight neo-Egyptian touch.

Architect Alcide Chaussé, decorator Emmanuel Briffa and sculptor Edouard Galea set to work, finding their inspiration in the great Ancient Egyptian temples. The Empress thus became a perfect example of late 1920s "atmospheric" decor, the goal of which was to place the audience in exotic surroundings.

The painted ceilings of the magnificent interior domes evoked the night sky that saw Tutankhamen enter the world and, on the walls, frescoes depicted life in Ancient Egypt. The original theatre, which consisted of a single room, seated 1,350 people.

In its early years, the Empress showed silent films and small vaudeville shows, like the city's other grand venues. Little by little, vaudeville died out, talking movies appeared, and the Great Depression dealt the Empress its final blow, leading to its closure in 1939. It was the beginning of a relentless decline that continues today.

In 1962, the theatre reopened to welcome the "Royal Follies" cabaret and part of the original decor was destroyed. The Empress was then transformed into a movie theatre in pure 1960s fashion, with rather gaudy red and blue fabric. The ceiling domes were perforated to make way for air ducts and replaced by a dropped ceiling, thus irreparably condemning the original design. The newly named "V" cinema was split in two. The Blue Room projected erotic films, which were quite popular in the 1970s, while art movies were shown in the Red Room. For twenty years, this neighbourhood cinema was a landmark for avant-garde work, but it experienced more financial problems in the late 1980s. Further conversions were planned under the direction of the new owners, the "Famous Player" group, but unfortunately in 1992 a serious fire devastated the interior, leading yet again to the theatre closing its doors.

Finally, the City of Montreal inherited this architectural jewel and has tried to save it through collaboration with various associations, such as the Empress Cultural Centre. The façade has been renovated and projects to convert it into a multicultural centre have been considered.

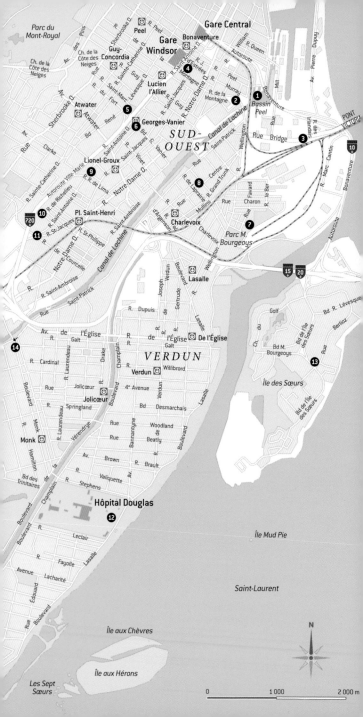

WEST CENTRAL
AND SOUTH-WEST

PEEL BASIN PANORAMA ❶

Take rue Mill in the Old Port
• Guided boat tours May to October at 1 pm and 3:30 pm, Saturday,
Sunday and public holidays, and daily from late June to early
September • The boats leave from quai du Marché Atwater south of
rue Saint-Ambroise and avenue Atwater
• Tel: 514 283 6054 and 1 888 773 8888
• Métro: Lionel-Groulx

*The best
view
of Montreal*

The Peel Basin, formed at the foot of the
Bonaventure highway (A-10) during
the regeneration of Canal de Lachine,
offers the most striking view of the downtown
skyscrapers. At dawn and dusk, the large
steel and glass towers are reflected in the calm waters, creating a beautiful
mirror effect. This is where the walking and cycle path connecting the Old
Port of Saint Louis Lake to the confluence of the Saint Lawrence River and
the Des Prairies River begins. What used to be one of the main hubs of North
American commerce has been transformed into a large elongated park,
11 kilometres of bliss. Floodlighting makes it possible to enjoy the flat paths
until midnight, which is perfect for warm summer evenings.

As you stroll along these peaceful riverbanks, it's hard to imagine that, until
the late 1960s, dozens of transport barges navigated this canal and passed
through its locks. Excavated from 1821 to 1824 to bypass the Lachine rapids
that so frightened the first explorers, the Lachine Canal played a central role
in the country's economic development during the Industrial Revolution.

From 1846 to the Second World War, some 600 businesses settled along
the canal, which served not only for transport but also as a water reservoir
to keep the factories running. All sorts of products were manufactured here,
ranging from textiles, coal, iron and steel to flour, wheat and sugar. For a
century, working-class neighbourhoods filled with a low-paid workforce
developed. The opening of the Saint Lawrence River to maritime transport
signalled the canal's decline. It was finally closed to navigation in 1970.
Residents had to wait until 2002 to see the canal opened to navigation again,
but this time for recreational boats only.

THE REMAINS OF GRIFFINTOWN

Saint Anne of Griffintown
Parc Sainte-Anne, still called Griffintown Saint Anne's park, corner of rue
de la Montagne and rue Wellington
• Métro: Bonaventure or Lucien-L'Allier

> *Phantom ruins of a vanished church*

Heading down rue de la Montagne towards the Saint Lawrence River, you come across a small, untended park at the corner of rue Wellington. As you approach you'll notice a few stone walls and some wooden benches bizarrely aligned in the same direction. Walk into the undergrowth to find a stele broken in two and the remains of a staircase. It's hard to imagine that this was once the heart of the Irish Catholic district of Griffintown. A plaque with an old photo unveils the mystery. We are at the ruins of Saint Anne's Church, or Sainte-Anne to the few French speakers who lived in this poor neighbourhood at the time.

The mid-19th century brought its share of immigrants, including a large number of Irish fleeing the 1847 famine. Penniless but having survived the dangers of crossing the Atlantic, they supplied cheap labour for the construction of the Lachine canal, the Victoria Bridge and the railway. Later, they were employed at the factories that were built along the canal banks. They lived in cramped slums that were regularly flooded by the nearby Saint Lawrence River when they weren't stricken by recurrent fires. Saint Anne's Church was built in 1854 to serve this growing population, and it quickly became the centre of community life in the neighbourhood. After the Second World War, the population of Griffintown declined. In the early 1960s, Mayor Jean Drapeau decided that it had no future as a residential neighbourhood. The bulldozers moved in, making way for an industrial zone and the Bonaventure highway. Having lost its parishioners, Saint Anne's Church couldn't escape demolition in 1970. The long abandoned vacant lot where the church once stood was recently made into a park. The monument's foundations were revealed and several benches were placed where the church pews once stood.

WHERE DOES GRIFFINTOWN'S NAME COME FROM?

In the early 19th century, the nuns of Hôtel-Dieu hospital rented a property in the former Faubourg des Récollets neighbourhood, known as the fief Nazareth, from Thomas McCord, a rich Irish property developer. In circumstances that remain obscure, the 99-year lease fell into the hands of Robert and Mary Griffin, who had a soap factory and employee housing built on the property. The exploited and impoverished workers soon owed Mrs Griffin so much money that the neighbourhood became known as Griffintown.

FORMER SQUARE GALLERY CHALET

128, rue Murray
• Métro: Bonaventure or Lucien-L'Allier

Art Deco urinals

Not far from Parc Sainte-Anne, at the end of rue Murray behind the parapets of the now blocked-off entrance to the Wellington Tunnel, stands the former square Gallery chalet, built in 1932.

At the time, the city had decided to equip its parks and squares with service buildings, urinals and "chalets" in order to improve the hygiene of the city's public areas while providing storage space for maintenance equipment and caretaker's lodges.

This period of construction, in the middle of an economic crisis, was also meant to provide as much work as possible for Montreal's unemployed.

Designed by architect David Jerome Spence, the square Gallery chalet is an example of Art Deco architecture. It is relatively well-preserved, as the numerous decorative motifs of its façade attest.

From 1973 to 1995, the chalet housed a community centre for disabled people, and today it is a commercial space. Projects to save and rehabilitate the park and this symbolic monument are being considered as part of the vast Griffintown development project.

Square Gallery was named in honour of Daniel Gallery, the district's city councillor from 1898 to 1910.

HOGAN BATH
2188, rue Wellington
• Métro: Charlevoix

The Hogan baths, also designed by architect David Jerome Spence, is an Art Deco structure built in 1931 next to Marguerite Bourgeoys park.

In 1998, the public baths were converted into eighteen flats with a shared roof-top terrace offering a beautiful view of the city centre.

SEBASTOPOL ROW HOUSES
422–444, rue Sébastopol
• Métro: Charlevoix

This "company housing", inspired by the British model, was built to house the specialized labour force of the Grand Trunk Railway of Canada (now the Canadian National Railway Company).

Grand Trunk Row was later renamed rue de Sébastopol, in memory of the Anglo-French victory over the Russian army in Crimea in 1855. The complex was composed of six houses, each containing four apartments, around a central boarding house. Today, only the three houses saved from the 1960s demolition still remain.

The vacant lot on the street was made into a pretty garden. The row of houses that was once in such a sorry state now stands quite proudly.

TO
PRESERVE FROM DESECRATION
THE REMAINS OF 6000 IMMIGRANTS
WHO DIED OF SHIP FEVER
A.D. 1847-8

THIS STONE
IS ERECTED BY THE WORKMEN
OF
MESS. PETO, BRASSEY & BETTS
EMPLOYED IN THE CONSTRUCTION
OF THE
VICTORIA BRIDGE
A.D. 1859

THE BLACK ROCK OF VICTORIATOWN

Rue Bridge towards Victoria Bridge, after rue Mill
• Bus line 74 (Bridge stop) / N°225

*Remembering
the Irish
immigrants*

I n 1847, the Great Irish Famine led to massive emigration to Canada. Weakened by the long trip and malnutrition, the immigrants arrived in poor condition. Typhus was a real threat. Sick immigrants were placed in quarantine on an island of the Saint Lawrence River north of Quebec, but those considered to be healthy were allowed to continue their voyage. When they arrived in Montreal, many had already fallen sick. Camps were quickly built at Windmill Point (now Victoriatown) to accommodate the victims of what was called "ship fever". Nearly 6,000 Irish immigrants perished in this improvised hospital run by the Sisters of Charity of Montreal (the Grey Nuns). The dead were promptly buried near the Saint Lawrence River.

Ten years later, during the excavations for the construction of the Victoria Bridge to connect Montreal Island to the South Shore, workmen discovered the remains. To pay homage to these unfortunate souls, a large stone originally taken from the river to build one of the bridge's piles was erected as a monument. It was engraved with the following words: "To preserve from desecration the remains of 6000 immigrants who died of ship fever A.D. 1847-8. This stone is erected by the workmen of Messrs Peto, Brassey & Betts, employed in the construction of the Victoria Bridge, A.D. 1859."

The "Irish rock", as it was called, weighs 30 tonnes and is 3 metres tall. Blackened by time and pollution, it is now known as the Black Rock. When a new body is discovered nearby, it is buried near this symbolic stone. In 1942, the Irish Ambassador declared that "Every time remains are discovered, a voice arises from the old earth."

In the early 1960s, rue Bridge, where the stone is located, had to be widened in preparation for Expo 67. But the Irish stone was not disturbed. Instead of moving it, the street was redesigned to include a central reservation. The descendants of Irish immigrants still come here to pay their respects.

At Windmill Point, a new neighbourhood, Goose Village, was built. It officially became Victoriatown in reference to the nearby Victoria Bridge. After the Irish, the Italians populated the six streets of this working-class neighbourhood near the factories of Lachine Canal. The housing was demolished in 1964; only the fire station, train station and Black Rock were spared. This industrial wasteland is now an inaccessible area between the Bonaventure highway and the railway tracks.

GEORGES VANIER GARDEN ❹

Corner of rue Saint-Jacques and rue Jean-d'Estrées
• Métro: Bonaventure or Lucien-L'Allier

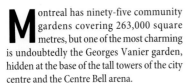

Tomatoes at the foot of skyscrapers

Montreal has ninety-five community gardens covering 263,000 square metres, but one of the most charming is undoubtedly the Georges Vanier garden, hidden at the base of the tall towers of the city centre and the Centre Bell arena.

Indeed, it's the most urban of these little gardens for the use of Montreal residents. The city's community gardens programme was started in 1975. Since 2002, each of the city's nineteen districts has been responsible for managing its respective gardens.

In some districts, a horticulturist visits the often novice gardeners to provide help and advice. The equipment, soil, watering supplies, tools, tables, fencing and ornamental flowers are all provided. An elected committee of volunteers runs the gardens, which are habitually opened on May 1st and closed on November 1st.

The Georges Vanier garden comprises sixty-three plots, each measuring 3.5 by 6 metres. They are rented by the year for the modest sum of $25 ($10 for the city and $15 for the committee).

The waiting lists are quite long for a plot in one of Montreal's community gardens, extremely popular since they were launched. Residents often have to wait several years before they can join the inner circle of urban gardeners. Of those who participate in community gardens, 40% do so first and foremost to grow fresh produce, while another 40% see it as a way to socialize with their gardening neighbours. For the remaining minority, gardening is simply a way to save money. Indeed, a good gardener can grow hundreds of dollars worth of vegetables each season. All the vegetable gardens are organic because the city

has banned the use of pesticides. The committees also strongly encourage composting.

At Georges Vanier, a sense of conviviality is kept alive through the morning coffee meetings held two or three times a year, the September corn roast and the annual picnic.

Contrary to common belief, the community gardens aren't just for retired people. Two groups seem to emerge: those 50 and over, but also young adults of 20 to 35. There's no age for growing green fingers!

MELVIN CHARNEY SCULPTURE GARDEN   ⑤

1918, boulevard René-Lévesque Ouest between rue Saint-Marc and rue du Fort
• Métro: Georges-Vanier

Dismantled architecture

Wedged between two ramps of the Ville-Marie highway, Melvin Charney park is actually an annex of the Canadian Centre for Architecture (CCA) on the opposite side of boulevard René-Lévesque.

The park is in fact a sculpture garden designed and built by the late artist and architect Melvin Charney between 1987 and 1991 on an abandoned lot.

Both urban garden and open-air museum, it is divided into several narrative sections: Orchard, Meadow, Arcade (mirror of Shaughnessy House, the central section of the CCA), the Esplanade, Belvedere and Allegorical Columns. Each of these columns refers to an element of the city that is still visible from the promontory at the other end of the park.

Inspired by what remains of this industrial zone of the past two centuries (the grain silos, the steeples of Sainte-Cunégonde church, and the last factory chimneys), "each sculpture refers to a piece of Montreal history, and the closer you get to the building, the more abstract they become", the mastermind behind these unusual gardens has explained.

Architecture, landscape and sculpture are brilliantly intertwined in this avant-garde setting where many local students like to take a break between classes.

TREE IN GEORGES-VANIER MÉTRO STATION ❻

On the Georges-Vanier station platform (orange line)
2040, rue St-Antoine Ouest

*An original
work of art*

Few people notice, but Georges-Vanier métro station, in the Petite Bourgogne district, houses an original work of art: the concrete pillar that appears to support the vault and light the platform towards Côte-Vertu is, in fact, a sculpture entitled *A Tree in the Park*.

Each of its "branches" contains a light which, unfortunately, doesn't always work. It's not that easy to replace a light bulb at a height of 12.8 metres!

This new kind of tree sprang from the imagination of artist Michel Dernuet of the Claude Théberge workshop. Sculptor Antoine D. Lamarche, of the same workshop, also participated in the project in 1976.

NEARBY

WORKERS OF MONK MÉTRO STATION

Not far from here, on the green line, monumental sculptures catch the eye of passers-by: two giant workers (over 6 metres tall) stand on each side of the

walkway inside Monk station. Both are in full swing, with one breaking stone and the other shovelling.

Inaugurated in 1978, the work is called *Pic et Pelle* (Pick and Shovel), after a Quebecois expression meaning "work hard".

It is signed by artist Germain Bergeron, who wanted to pay tribute to all the workers who participated in the construction of the Montreal métro in the 1960s and 1970s. It's said that the orange-coloured metal used for the two sculptures comes from recycled street lamps.

MAISON SAINT-GABRIEL GARDENS ❼

2146, place Dublin, Pointe-Saint-Charles
• Métro: Charlevoix • Tel: 514 935 8136
• Guided tours of Maison Saint-Gabriel: about 1 hour
• Mid-January to mid-December, Tuesday to Sunday, 1 pm to 5 pm,
open till 6 pm in summer • Closed mid-December to mid-January and on
Monday
• Admission: adults $10, children $3 • In summer, admission and tours
are free on Tuesday and Wednesday at 5 pm

In New France fashion ...

Although many have heard of Maison Saint-Gabriel, the famous home of the King's Wards* that provides great insight into life in New France, few have explored the gardens surrounding it. Indeed, several gardens have been planted around the house in the past ten years to recreate the period of the first settlers.

The first of these, the **Farmhouse Garden**, follows rural traditions by combining flowers, aromatic herbs and vegetables, thus perpetuating the spirit of the 17th century. Popular vegetables of the period (turnips, rutabagas, cabbages, Jerusalem artichokes, salsifies, carrots, beans, etc.) are laid out in well-organized rows separated by flowers (marigolds, nasturtiums, daylilies, bergamots, poppies, musk-mallows, roses, pansies, dame's rocket, hollyhocks, bellflowers, etc.). A few steps away, herbs fill the air with their

subtle scents: thyme, lovage, lavender, coriander, spearmint, sage, camomile, chives, chervil, and more. With such surroundings, it's hard to believe you're in the middle of the city.

Entrance to the museum is through the **Sharecroppers' Garden**, which explores the site's history, theme by theme, from the clearing of the property to the arrival of urbanization. It pays tribute to the women who ran the farm of the Congregation of Notre Dame. Several works of contemporary art, relating to the past, have been magnificently integrated into the garden.

But our favourite garden is the last one under the property's hundred-year-old trees. In the undergrowth, you'll find numerous indigenous plants of Quebec: alpine currant, Canadian elderberry, withrod, highbush cranberry, and other ferns and herbaceous plants. They are all indicated on interpretive signs. And as the exploration of plants and flowers naturally leads to the discovery of new words, a **Poetry Path** invites visitors to discover francophone and anglophone poets who have written about nature and made their mark on Canadian literature, such as Anne Hébert or Margaret Atwood.

*Or *filles du roi*, girls recruited in France as wives for the single men of the colony.

> Every Sunday in summer, a guided tour takes place from 12 noon to 5 pm to learn more about the plants and flowers of the period. Artisans, actors and musicians participate in the festivities, and let's not forget the tasting of local products. This is also the only place where you can buy *Les Métayères* cheese, an exclusive creation of Du Champ à la Meule dairy. The sales help to fund the museum and its activities.

WRESTLING IN CHURCH

❽

Église Saint-Charles Borromée
2115, rue du Centre
• Métro: Charlevoix
• Saturday night at 7 pm, admission $5
• Check the dates for wrestling nights • Tel: 514 932 5335

> *American wrestling as a form of rehabilitation*

L ocated at the heart of the Pointe-Saint-Charles neighbourhood, the basement of Saint Charles church is the venue nearly every Saturday night for an activity you don't commonly find in a Catholic church: wrestling!

For two hours, thirty adult professionals and neighbourhood youths confront one another in a series of WTA (Wrestling Titan Association) wrestling performances.

Michel Piché, who initiated the project in 1994, was able to convince the parish priest of the time of the advantages of creating a wrestling school in the church basement and of organizing performances there. Convinced that this simulated, disciplined violence was a true way to escape the street violence that was a common occurrence in this underprivileged neighbourhood, one of the city's poorest, the priest gave Piché his blessing.

American wrestling thus became a form of rehabilitation, allowing youths to fight against the rough realities of the neighbourhood.

Sporting a leather coat, several tattoos and a Mohawk, Michel Piché, alias The Scorpion Killer, believes this sport has helped a lot of troubled teens.

When it comes to discipline, he never wavers one basic rule: no good grades, no wrestling.

At 7 pm, a couple of hundred people push into the room: adults and children of all ages run between the rows of plastic orange chairs. Inflation seems to be slower here than elsewhere and hot dogs still only cost $1.25.

Among the wrestlers, look out for Kevin the Criminal, Bulldozer, Dinamicke, Voltage, Black Jack and Frankie Boy, a 15-year-old who became the king of the world on the night we were there.

PARISIAN LAUNDRY'S ART DECO PORTICO

3550, rue Saint-Antoine Ouest
- Tel: 514 989 1056
- Tuesday to Friday, 12 noon to 6 pm, Saturday, 12 noon to 5 pm
- Private tours by reservation
- Métro: Lionel-Groulx

Art and industry in the same league

As its name suggests, for nearly seventy years the Parisian Laundry was home to a commercial laundry specializing in cleaning linen and uniforms for the city's leading hotels and restaurants.

Nick Tedeschi, a Montreal businessman and art collector, bought the building in 2000. A true patron of the arts, he spent nearly $2 million on its restoration, turning it into a contemporary art gallery. The laundry's industrial nature was preserved during this conversion, making it the extraordinary and rather astounding place it is today. Concrete floors, wooden and steel beams, large windows – all these original elements were preserved, including the Art Deco portico and the Parisian Laundry sign carved in grey stone, of course.

With its 1,400 square metres (15,000 square feet) of space on three floors, its high ceilings and profuse light, the gallery offers an exceptional exhibition space.

A dozen exhibitions are held here every year to present living artists from Canada and abroad, but also communal projects and works by art students. Multimedia pieces are shown in the Bunker, a large, dark room in the basement.

A marvelous reconversion, the Parisian Laundry perfectly illustrates the close relationship between industrial and contemporary art. With such sites as the Darling Foundry, the Belgo and Usine C, Montreal seems to have made this relationship a distinguishing feature of the city.

MUSÉE DES ONDES ÉMILE BERLINER

1050, rue Lacasse
- Métro: Place Saint-Henri
- Tel: 514 932 9663 • Admission: $3 for adults, $2 for children
- Open all year, Friday to Sunday, 2 pm to 5 pm

His Master's Voice

Founded by a group of techies, the Émile Berliner museum defines itself as a place for the conservation and exhibition of all objects relating to the history of the production, reproduction, capturing and diffusion of sound.

Its collections, on the second floor of one of RCA Victor's former industrial buildings, include an incredible variety of gramophones, phonographs, radios, televisions, tape recorders, microphones and thousands of vinyl records.

Every year in the exhibition room, visitors discover a different theme highlighting part of the collection. It's the chance to discover objects that remind us of childhood, and for younger ones to discover devices they've never seen.

When the museum opened to the public on January 24, 1996, it already owned a hundred objects. Since then, and thanks to the generosity of more than 500 contributors, it now has more than 30,000.

The old machine collecting dust in your basement could be a treasure for the museum, whose purpose is also to preserve this unique and essential cultural heritage for generations to come.

On the guided tours, visitors can not only admire these machines from the past, but also listen to the music of yesteryear.

ÉMILE BERLINER, INVENTOR OF THE GRAMOPHONE AND THE RECORD

Émile Berliner invented the first microphone for Graham Bell's telephone, but more importantly he was the inventor of the gramophone and the record. The German engineer, who first immigrated to the United States, set up his company in Montreal in 1900. Along with his company, he registered an image that would become the symbol of recording: Nipper the dog, listening to a gramophone and recognizing "His Master's Voice". English painter Francis Barraud created this icon, which was used for over seventy years.

The first records were engraved on only one side, with Nipper's image on the other. It wasn't until 1908 that both sides began to be engraved. The baritone Joseph Saucier supposedly had the privilege of recording the first record in Montreal, in 1904, with the song *La Marseillaise*.

LOUIS CYR

LOUIS CYR MONUMENT

Place des Hommes-Forts, junction of rue Saint-Jacques and rue Saint-Antoine

• Métro: Place Saint-Henri

> **Tribute to the strongest man in the world**

This imposing bronze statue in the Saint-Henri neighbourhood is rather curious. Its curved shape and deliberate exaggeration of the subject is reminiscent of the work of Colombian artist Fernando Botero, although it is by sculptor Robert Pelletier and was erected here in 1970.

Louis Cyr was easily the strongest man in the world at the time, and perhaps the strongest that ever lived. Novelist and scriptwriter Paul Ohl, his biographer, described him as "a man with the strength of ten men, whom no Hercules ever defeated … and who pushed the doors of his country wide open".

Born in 1863 in a little village of the Montérégie region between Montreal and the US border, the young Cyprien-Noé Cyr was endowed from his early childhood with uncommon strength, which he put to use working in lumber camps and on the family farm from the age of 12.

The story goes that one day, after he had immigrated to Lowell, Massachusetts, with his family, he freed a cart stuck up to its axles in the mud using his sheer strength and broad shoulders. Impressed, the driver invited the young man to participate in his first strongman competition in Boston. At just 18, he lifted a horse off the ground!

His career was launched. The young Cyprien-Noé became Louis Cyr, after his Acadian ancestor,* choosing a name that was much easier to pronounce in English.

In the late 19th century, strongman contests, the precursors of weightlifting, were very popular. They took the form of challenges as the athletes took turns to confront one another in a series of special lifts. Louis Cyr became a legend.

The Canadian Samson, as he was known at the time, drew crowds. In 1892, at age 29, he was proclaimed "the strongest man in the world" at a competition in London.

During his 23-year career, he travelled around the United States, Canada, England and Wales, giving over 2,500 strongman performances and participating in more than 1,000 circus shows. Some of his records still stand today, such as that of holding back two pairs of horses weighing a total of more than 2 tonnes for 55 seconds, or lifting a total of 7.5 tonnes in seven events in less than two hours!

He died in Montreal in 1912 at the age of 49 and is buried in the Saint-Jean-de-Matha cemetery in Lanaudière, where he lived until his death. His name is deeply engraved in Quebec's popular heritage.

*Acadians are the descendants of 17th-century French who settled in Acadia, a colony of New France.

DOUGLAS HOSPITAL SCULPTURE GARDEN ⑫

6875, boulevard LaSalle, Verdun
• Métro: Angrignon

*Art against
mental illness*

I n Montreal, you'll find one of the city's most beautiful sculpture gardens at a psychiatric hospital. This original idea came from one of the nurses at the Mental Health University Institute of McGill University, a hospital at the leading edge of international research, generally known as "The Douglas".

Edward Cohen, an art lover, built this sculpture garden through charm, conviction and determination. Indeed, he had to persuade reputable sculptors to donate one of their works so that patients, employees and visitors could benefit from a relaxing environment in the hospital grounds.

His goal has been successfully reached because, since 2001, when the first two Esther Wertheimer sculptures arrived, twenty works have been donated, each more amazing than the last.

Today, the Douglas Foundation is still looking for new donations to enrich its collection. In exchange, it offers a tax-deductible receipt for 50% of the value of the work. To be accepted, the sculptures must be the work of a professional artist, pose no danger, stand up to the Quebec winters, and most importantly blend in with the park's philosophy by bringing comfort and hope to the patients.

MIES VAN DER ROHE GAS STATION

Île des Sœurs (Nuns' Island)
201, rue Berlioz
• Tel: 514 766 4301
• Bus lines 12 and 168 (Berlioz/ L'île-des-Sœurs stop)

A successful conversion

Few Montreal residents know that rue Berlioz, on Nuns' Island, is home to one of the most original constructions of famous German-American architect Ludwig Mies van der Rohe (1886–1969).

In the 1960s, the Chicago-based architect designed several projects for Montreal. Although the best known is undoubtedly the Westmount Square residential complex, he also worked on the development of Nuns' Island, which was in a full real-estate boom following the opening of Champlain Bridge in 1962. He designed three residential tower blocks and a gas station for the island. The station was built from 1967 to 1968 and remained in service for forty years, until it was shut down permanently in 2008. The building, characterized by the elegance and sobriety of its architectural composition and the use of quality materials, is composed of a large rectangular roof supported by a steel structure delineating three separate spaces: the reception area, the garage and the cashier's booth.

Everything at this station was signed Mies van der Rohe: the design of the fuel pumps, the Esso sign, the storage units and the furniture. The original pumps were replaced in 1975 and, over the decades, various renovations modified the building, but never erased its original appearance.

After it closed, the gas station was listed as a historic monument in 2009 and converted to an "inter-generational community centre", the first of its kind in Montreal. Opened in February 2012, it provides activities and services for young people from 12 to 17 as well as the over-50s, including computer and cooking classes, tutoring sessions, and more. What a beautiful example of a successful conversion.

MUSÉE DE LACHINE SCULPTURE GARDEN 🄬

1, chemin du Musée, Lachine district
• Métro: Angrignon then bus 110 Ouest westbound
• Tel: 514 634 3478
• Sculp'tour: 9 am to 4:30 pm Wednesday to Sunday, from early April to late November. These free walking or cycling guided tours are a unique way to discover contemporary sculpture (reservation only)

On the banks of the Saint Lawrence River, just 10 kilometres from the city centre, history, art and nature coincide at one of Canada's largest sculpture gardens.

Art along the riverbank

Surprisingly, many Montreal residents still aren't aware of its existence.

The Lachine Museum sculpture garden begins at the LeBer-LeMoyne House, a former fur-trading post dating from 1669, and possesses over fifty works exhibited in three parks: René-Lévesque park along the canal, the riverside parks along the Saint Lawrence, and the museum's main site.

You can visit the garden in three different ways: by foot, by bike or by following a treasure hunt designed especially for families. Every sculpture along the tour has its own informative plaque providing the name of the artist and the history of its design and construction. Here, you'll find works by such renowned artists as André Fournelle, Michel Goulet, David Moore and Bill Vazan, Lisette Lemieux, and Robert Roussil.

René-Lévesque park, the largest of the three exhibition areas, covers over 14 hectares of the peninsula between the end of the Lachine Canal cycle path and the river. In the early morning mist or the rays of the setting sun, its twenty-two sculptures blend into their natural surroundings, which vary with the light and the seasons. Created in 1985 to bring together the city's residents and its artists, this park has grown richer with every year.

EAST CENTRAL AND EAST MONTREAL

FORMER BATHHOUSE GÉNÉREUX ❶

Écomusée du Fier Monde
2050, rue Amherst, corner of Ontario
• Métro: Berri-UQAM
• Tel: 514 528 8444

A superb example of Art Deco architecture

What could be a more original setting for a museum dedicated to industrial history and culture than a swimming pool? Take a closer look, however, and you'll see that these two entities are more closely related than you'd think. Both take you back to another era, that of the Industrial Revolution, the first factories, a booming industry and a rapidly developing working class. The former Généreux bathhouse, which became the home of the Écomusée du Fier Monde in 1995, has its rightful place in this new urban fabric. A magnificent example of 1920s architecture, the bathhouse is a reminder of the city's efforts to improve the living conditions of working-class neighbourhoods where baths and showers were still a luxury.

The Écomusée du Fier Monde is an industrial history museum whose field of interest lies within the triad of work, industry and culture. It highlights the history and heritage of Montreal's Centre-Sud (south-central) district, which was a veritable microcosm of Canada's Industrial Revolution from the second half of the 19th century to the late 1950s. Through exhibitions of old photographs, tools, period manufactured products, and more, a guided tour of this museum plunges visitors into the daily life of thousands of working-class families of the epic industrial era. And what can be said about the sumptuous decor of this building that experienced glory, then

abandonment, before finding a new lease of life? The Généreux bathhouse, named after a city councillor at its 1927 inauguration, is a beautiful example of Art Deco architecture, with the clean lines of its façade, interior beams arched like the hull of a boat, and numerous openings that let in the light. The architect, Jean-Omer Marchand, supposedly found his inspiration in the Butte-aux-Cailles swimming pool in Paris, which was also in a working-class neighbourhood and was completed by architect Louis Bonnier a few years earlier. The Généreux bathhouse quickly welcomed countless bathers. Since the 1940s, the pool has been home to a swimming club. The elite athletes of this growing sport trained with the Montreal Aquatic Club until 1977, when the club moved to the new Olympic facilities of the Claude Robillard Centre. Little by little, the bathers deserted the older, outdated baths for the city's new larger swimming pools. In 1992, heating and plumbing problems forced the Généreux to close. After renovation work led by architect Felice Vaccaro, the bathhouse became a museum and reopened to the public in 1996.

MICHEL DE BROIN'S "REVOLUTIONS"

Parc Maisonneuve-Cartier next to Papineau station
• Métro: Papineau

> *Identity*
> *of the Montreal*
> *landscape*

Revolution: the rotation of a body around its central axis or around another body. That's the dictionary definition. Try to follow this curved staircase that seems to go on forever and your eyes will get lost in an infinite rotation that "defies gravity and the subjective reference of up and down".

Measuring 8 metres high by 5 metres wide, this original work by sculptor Michel de Broin is meant to be a reflection of the Montreal landscape. The artist took his inspiration from the famous exterior wrought-iron staircases found around the city streets and at emblematic sites nearby. He imagines this form "resonating with the metal structures of Jacques-Cartier Bridge, then heading off to take a twirl with the rides at La Ronde amusement park, before finally taking its place here like a bouquet emerging from the flower beds".

The work is made from marine-grade aluminium, strongly resistant to corrosion and more solid than standard alloys. This sculpture, a competition winner, was added to the city's collection of public art in 2003. Michel de Broin, a Montrealer born in 1970, is mainly known for the works he has on display in public spaces.

The mission of the Montreal Public Art Bureau is to conserve, acquire, showcase and promote the works of the city's collection of public art, which includes more than 300 works found throughout the territory. Some are fully independent exterior works, while others are integral parts of the city's architecture. Since 1989, and the establishment of the public art action plan, over thirty works have come to enrich Montreal's collective heritage, and forty others have undergone conservation or restoration work.

THE SAQ EXHIBITION CENTRE

903, avenue De Lorimier
• Tel: 514 254 6000, ext. 6245
• Open Wednesday, Thursday and Friday, 12 noon to 5 pm; Saturday and Sunday, 9:30 am to 5 pm, admission free
• Métro: Papineau

The remains of the Patriots prison

The history of the former Patriots prison, at the foot of Jacques-Cartier Bridge, is closely related to a bloody period of Canadian history: the 1837 and 1838 Patriots rebellions.

This neoclassical monument was built from 1831 to 1840 to house the new prison, named "Au-Pied-du-Courant" (literally, at the foot of the current) due to its proximity to the Saint Lawrence River. The buildings took in their first prisoners, including several hundred Patriots, before they were even completed. Twelve of them were executed by hanging right in front of the prison entrance, the only section of the old defensive wall still standing today.

Marked by this event, the establishment was commonly referred to as the Prison-des-Patriotes. After an extension and other modifications, the building was finally abandoned in 1912 in favour of a larger detention centre in the north of the island, the Bordeaux prison. In 1921, the Liquor Commission set up its headquarters in the old prison and the cells were turned into wine cellars. The commission's successor, the Société des Alcools du Québec (SAQ), is still based here.

In 2003, the SAQ opened an exhibition centre for the public. The permanent exhibit in the basement comprehensively recounts the 1837 and 1838 rebellions, as well as the living conditions of the prisoners of the period. It's easy to imagine the cells as they once were – the rings used to attach the prisoners are still there.

NEARBY

THE PATRIOTS MONUMENT

The Patriots monument, designed in 1926 by Alfred Laliberté, has stood opposite the former prison since 1993. It consists of a bronze sculpture symbolizing Liberty with broken wings standing on a grey granite pedestal. On each of the pedestal's three sides is a carved bronze medallion depicting a Patriot: De Lorimier, Papineau and Nelson.

TU QUANG PAGODA ❹

2176, rue Ontario Est
• Métro: Frontenac • Tel: 514 525 8122
• Open to the public on Sunday, 10 am to 12 noon

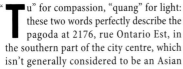

*Discover
Vietnam
in Montreal*

"**T**u" for compassion, "quang" for light: these two words perfectly describe the pagoda at 2176, rue Ontario Est, in the southern part of the city centre, which isn't generally considered to be an Asian neighbourhood. The city's Vietnamese community of around 30,000 people is spread out through many of Montreal's neighbourhoods and suburbs. This temple, inaugurated in 1985, ten years after the exodus of the first "boat people", is thus a beautiful example of the city's multiculturalism.

The large white statue that sits imposingly in the middle of the entrance courtyard is a representation of Bodhisattva Quan Am, the only female Buddha worshiped by Buddhists all over the world as the saviour Buddha. According to the "Great Vehicle" (Mahayana) branch of Buddhism, she refused Nirvana and returned to the world of the suffering to help mankind as a sort of guardian angel.

Encircling Quan Am, eighteen other statues organized in two separate rows represent the Arhats, noble beings that have attained the last level of wisdom. The sumptuous interior with its abundance of red and gold reflects the grandeur of the imperial courts. On the second floor, in the room of worship, the three Buddhas watch over the visitors: Dia Tang, protector of the dead; Shakyamuni, the historic Buddha; and, once again, Quan Am, the female Bodhisattva. On Sunday, from 10 am to 12 noon, the temple is open to both believers and non-believers alike. You are simply requested to remove your shoes at the entrance, not to interrupt the services, not to eat or drink, and to turn off your mobile phone.

OTHER VIETNAMESE PLACES OF WORSHIP IN MONTREAL

The multi-denominational Vietnamese community is generally divided among three religions: Buddhism, Catholicism and Caodaiism (see page 117). You can attend Vietnamese Catholic mass on Sunday at 10:30 am and 5 pm at Église Saint-Philippe, also called Saints-Martyrs-du-Vietnam, which is located at 1420, rue Bélanger. Or you can visit the Cao Dai Temple, which was established in a former synagogue at 7161, rue Saint-Urbain.

The selection of Buddhist temples is much larger: Montreal has more than thirty, including seven Vietnamese pagodas. The oldest of them is the Quan Am pagoda at 3781, avenue de Courtrai, where services are held on Sunday from 10 am to 12 noon, and followed by a vegetarian meal served in the basement.

To truly get into the spirit, don't miss the celebration of Tet, the Vietnamese New Year, which is held in late January to early February on the first day of the lunar calendar.

IMUSÉE

Pavillon d'Éducation Communautaire Hochelaga-Maisonneuve
1691, boulevard Pie-IX
• Tel: 514 596 4488
• Tuesday to Saturday, 10 am to 5 pm
• Admission: $7
• Métro: Pie-IX

> **Computer history as told by geeks**

Who remembers the Apple Lisa, the first computer with a graphic interface, delivered with a mouse and launched in 1983, before the famous Macintosh?

It was to revive our collective computer history that the iMusée was set up in 2010. At its origin was a group of computer geeks from the Pavillon d'Éducation Communautaire Hochelaga-Maisonneuve, a community education centre.

Despite the fact that computers were the primary technical revolution of the late 20th century, we know little about their history. This museum fills in the gaps!

The visit begins in the stairwell, where panels retrace the steps of the internet

adventure, from the 1960s to today. Then come rooms filled with various, and sometimes surprising, objects. In the first section, "prehistory", you'll find a Chinese suanpan (abacus), oscilloscopes, perforated cards and the first computers, including an IBM 5100 with a screen smaller than that of a smartphone and which cost $19,000 at the time!

In the adjacent multimedia room, a short film retraces the main stages in the development of information processing. Next, you'll find the "modern" machines dating from the 1970s to today, most of which now appear ancient: Osborne, Commodore, Tandy, and the first Apple computers.

PLAY VIDEO GAMES AT YOUR LEISURE!
The museum visit ends with the video game console exhibit: Atari 2600, Sega Master System, Odyssey 2, PS1, Atari Jaguar, etc. And to top it all, they still work ...

GUIDO NINCHERI'S HOME STUDIO

1832, boulevard Pie-IX
• Visits organized by Château Dufresne (2929, avenue Jeanne-d'Arc at
the corner of Pie-IX and Sherbrooke)
• Métro: Pie-IX

> ## And
> there was light!

In this multicultural residential neighbourhood, you can't help but notice the house at 1832, boulevard Pie-IX, with its symmetrical façade of beige brick and its monumental arch of windows.

For more than seventy years, this building was home to the various studios of master glass artist Guido Nincheri. It witnessed the creation of some 5,000 stained-glass windows that are now on display in nine Canadian provinces and the six states of New England.

Nincheri, born in Italy, studied art at the Fine Arts Academy in Florence and immigrated to Montreal in 1914, after a short stay in Boston. His first job was with decorator Henri Perdriau, where he learned the art of stained glass. In 1925, he set up his own studio on the ground floor of the house on boulevard Pie-IX, which the Dufresne brothers had recently acquired. These rich businessmen soon became his patrons.

In 1932, he moved into the annex that had been built in the courtyard, but he didn't own the house until 1966.

The studio continued to operate even after the artist's death in 1973. Matteo Martinaro, one of the artist's followers, directed the studio until its definitive closure in 1996. Since then, it has hardly changed and now, after fifteen years when nothing much happened, the studio has been opened to the public. Some of the tours are even led by Roger Nincheri, the master artist's grandson and a great admirer of his grandfather's work.

During the visit you'll discover drawing boards, sketches, brushes, various cutting tools and the impressive kiln used to bake the pieces of glass. A few

colourful pieces have been placed here and there, giving the impression they are still waiting to be used for a window in one of the 200 North American churches beautified by the artist.

It is easy to imagine him in the 1950s, in these narrow rooms with high ceilings, instructing his ten employees.

The drawings are projected onto the wall, the measurements are taken, the glass is cut, and the colours are applied …

If it weren't for the dust and hopelessly cold oven, you would almost believe the studio was still in operation.

LES PETITS BAIGNEURS OF MORGAN BATHHOUSE

❼

1875, avenue Morgan
- Métro: Pie-IX
- Tel: 514 872 6657
- Admission free

"

A testimony to past splendour

I n Montreal, the construction of public bathhouses began in the late 19th century. As many people didn't have a bathroom in their home, the city decided to provide facilities for personal cleanliness and hygiene.

The imposing Morgan Bathhouse is one of the most beautiful buildings in Montreal. It was part of the luxurious and rather self-indulgent Maisonneuve development, which was a town in its own right until 1918 and a flagship of Quebec's manufacturing industry.

The construction of the bathhouse, inaugurated in May, 1916, was initially estimated to cost $30,000, but the final cost soared to $300,000, a fortune at the time, most notably due to the building's flamboyant façade.

Its designer, Marius Dufresne, aimed high, finding his inspiration in public bathhouses on 23rd street in New York and at Manhattan's Grand Central Terminal. Dufresne also borrowed the idea from a Boston bathhouse of including a gym on the upper floor. From 1920 to 1960, the gym served as a training facility for Montreal's police academy.

On the façade, around the inscription "Maissonneuve, Bain et Gymnase" (Maissonneuve, Bath and Gym), you'll find three sculptures in the round (three-dimensional) by Arthur Dubord: a man flanked by two horses, a naiad and a gymnast. In an alcove at the centre are *Les Petits Baigneurs* (The Little Bathers), a bronze by famous Quebec sculptor Alfred Laliberté.

Although the exterior hasn't been changed, the interior has unfortunately undergone several alterations over the decades. Renovation work has led to the removal of decorative elements, such as the columns and terraces that once surrounded the pool, as well as the private showers and baths once used by the neighbourhood's working-class residents.

CHÂTEAU DUFRESNE NUDES   **8**

2929, avenue Jeanne-d'Arc (corner of Pie-IX and Sherbrooke)
• Métro: Pie-IX • Tel: 514 259 9201
• Open Wednesday to Sunday, 10 am to 5 pm
• Guided tours in French at 1:30 pm and 3:30 pm on Saturday and
Sunday only, reservation not required
• Adults $8, children $4.50, family of four $18.50; combined tickets
available for Olympic Stadium or Guido Nincheri studio

*Covered
then rediscovered*

Château Dufresne was built between 1915 and 1918 by Oscar and Marius Dufresne, two pillars of Montreal's flourishing francophone bourgeoisie of the early 20th century. Oscar was a prosperous shoe manufacturer, while Marius was a leading businessman who participated in the urbanization and development of Maisonneuve.

The two brothers had the curious idea of building their respective living quarters in a mirror arrangement. Indeed, the two homes, each with over twenty rooms, are joined symmetrically within a single, individual residence.

A visit to their home plunges you into the elegant and opulent world of the well-to-do of the period. Château Dufresne follows the principles of Beaux-Arts architecture, a monumental yet elegant style. Architect Jules Renard supposedly drew his inspiration from Versailles' Petit Trianon. The view from the large wrought-iron gate on rue Sherbrooke is striking: the harmony of the refined façade highlighted by tall, decorative columns facing a beautiful French-style park. The richness of the interior decor of the Dufresne residence also holds its share of surprises. From the small sitting rooms to the reception halls, the imposing foyers to the more private oriental smoking room, and the offices to the tranquil winter gardens, every room is decorated in a different style according to its function and the atmosphere that the first owners wanted to create. Take time to admire the friezes, fireplaces, exotic woodwork, Italian marble staircases and, above all, the frescoes and stained-glass windows created by grand master Guido Nincheri. The Dufresne brothers contributed to his fame by entrusting him with the decoration of their luxurious home, then later by providing him with his own studio. Nincheri's paintings adorn several walls and ceilings throughout the residence, from the small boudoir to the reception hall, without forgetting the stairwell and several rooms upstairs. Unfortunately, nearly all the period stained-glass windows were destroyed during the building's dark years.

In 1948, after the death of the last Dufresne brother to live in the château, the sumptuous residence was sold to the Fathers of the Holy Cross. They converted it into a traditional day school which later became Collège Sainte-Croix. Countless changes spoiled the interior. They even covered some of Nincheri's allegorical frescoes, as they were deemed to be too suggestive for such a religious and educational institution.

This was notably the case of the reception hall ceiling, which was covered by a work in which love was represented by nudes. Shocked, the monks quickly hid the fresco beneath a layer of paint.

In 1957, the religious community handed the house over to the City of Montreal, which left the site unoccupied. The Museum of Contemporary Art took up residence here in 1965, but then moved to the Expo 67 International Art Gallery in the Cité du Havre district in 1968. Château Dufresne then went through its darkest period. Deserted, with no maintenance, heating or caretaking, it was subjected to great damage caused by weather and vandalism. In 1976, Jean Drapeau, the mayor of Montreal, took patron of the arts David M. Stewart on a private tour of the residence and convinced him to restore the home, which had recently been listed as a historic monument. Forty-two blueprints and drawings by Marius Dufresne, along with period photographs, were used to restore the site as accurately as possible. The nudes of the reception hall saw the light of day once again.

Although the original furnishings were purchased from the estate of Edna Sauriol Dufresne, Marius' widow, in the 1970s, the current museum didn't open to the public until 1999.

LESLIE HANCOCK GARDEN ❾

Montreal Botanical Garden
4101, rue Sherbrooke Est
• Métro: Pie-IX
• Tel: 514 872 1400

In the realm of the Ericaceae

This is one of the botanical garden's most well-kept secrets. At the heart of the 75 hectares of this Montreal gem, created in 1931 by Brother Marie Victorin, a small yet unique garden is concealed.

Until the mid-20th century, it was commonly believed that rhododendrons couldn't survive Canada's rigorous climate. But thanks to horticulturist Leslie Hancock (1892–1977), more and more Canadians can now cultivate them. One day, Leslie Hancock, a soldier, professor and deputy as well as a horticulturalist, discovered a passion for ericaceous plants, those acidic soil-loving shrubs of which heather, azaleas, and rhododendrons are the most popular representatives. As a specialist of their cultivation in less favourable climates, he was invited to come to Montreal and design an Ericacetum at the botanical garden. It was inaugurated in 1976 as the Ericaceae Garden, and later renamed the Leslie Hancock Garden in 1986.

Like a precious pearl, the garden is set in a ring of conifers that protects it from the wind and, curiously, the sun. In winter, when the temperature climbs above zero, the leaves that had curled up to protect themselves from the cold unfold and the plant starts to "perspire". As the frozen ground makes it impossible for them to replenish this loss of water, the rhododendron's leaves (especially those of the large-leaved varieties) begin to turn red. The conifers limit the damage by filtering the sun's rays.

This barrier also helps to keep the snow in the centre, which protects the plants from frost.

The best time to visit this garden is in spring. The flowering season, which lasts from April to early July, is an explosion of bright colours ranging from creamy white to incandescent red, and from orange-tinted purples to bright and soft pinks. After the flowering, new leaves appear in green, blue and grey tones.

In October, the shrubs ignite in the golden, purple and scarlet tones of autumn.

JARDIN TIKI

10

5300, rue Sherbrooke Est
• Métro: Assomption
• Tel: 514 254 4173

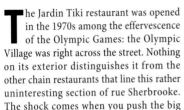

One of Montreal's temples of kitsch

The Jardin Tiki restaurant was opened in the 1970s among the effervescence of the Olympic Games: the Olympic Village was right across the street. Nothing on its exterior distinguishes it from the other chain restaurants that line this rather uninteresting section of rue Sherbrooke. The shock comes when you push the big brass handle and open the door to find a bridge over a small pond where large turtles frolic with dinosaur figurines and plastic sharks. An enormous, dangerous-looking red dragon looks down from above. Big lamps in the most improbable of shapes and strings of shells and grossly stylized tropical fish hang from the ceiling of the dining area. Welcome to one of Montreal's temples of kitsch, or more precisely of Polynesian kitsch.

In the 1950s, the numerous North Americans who had gone to Hawaii looking for paradise lost returned to the continent, bringing the island's folklore of bamboo huts, *aloha* shirts, exotic beverages and statues of local divinities with them. At once a lifestyle and decorative style, Polynesian pop (or Tiki culture) rapidly developed along the California coast, as dozens of Tiki bars popped up. The popularity of the Tiki god quickly spread throughout the country and into Canada. Montreal succumbed to the fad when Steve Crane, a B-movie Hollywood actor, opened the second restaurant of his Kon Tiki chain (after the one in Beverly Hills) in the Sheraton-Mont-Royal Hotel on rue Peel. When it closed in 1981, some of the furniture and decoration from the restaurant landed here, at the Jardin Tiki.

As for the food, the Chinese-American buffet appeals more for its abundance than for its gastronomy, but the fabulous exotic cocktails (in green, yellow, pink or blue) copiously garnished with tropical fruit and served in huge glasses – or even in a pineapple or coconut – make up for it.

CANADIAN FORCES LOGISTICS MUSEUM ⓫

6560, rue Hochelaga
• Open Wednesday to Sunday, 10 am to 4 pm
• We strongly recommend phoning in advance to ensure the curator (the museum's only employee) is available
• Admission free • Tel: 514 252 2777, ext. 2241
• Métro: Langelier

A museum in the barracks

First, you'll have to pass the control barrier of the Longue-Pointe military base before being able to visit this uncommon museum. Once you've shown your ID, you're asked to go directly to the former chapel, which was both Catholic (Saint-Michel) and Protestant (Sainte-Barbara) and in use until 1972 when the museum took over.

A stained-glass window and a cross still mark the building's former religious function. The museum's collection covers the activities of the Canadian Forces from the Boer War (1899–1902) to today.

Although the former Royal Canadian Ordnance Corps Museum (RCOCM), now the Canadian Forces Logistics Museum, includes the expected exhibits about weapons (some of which date from the 19th century), there is much more to be discovered here.

Nearly 2,000 objects in all are presented, each related to the supply of equipment needed for combat, training, and peace-keeping operations all over the world.

Some of the exhibits you'll discover are a beautiful collection of uniforms, some of which were created by Yves Saint-Laurent; various military decorations, including the famous German iron crosses from the Second World War; countless tools; and even a 1957 Triumph 500cc motorcycle, in perfect condition, no less, as it only has 3 kilometres on the clock!

A couple of the more moving objects are a greetings card made

from a corned beef tin and a 1940 military-issue sewing kit commonly called "the housewife".

The visit continues outside with the military vehicles, notably a 34 tonne Sherman tank, an East German T-72 tank built in the ex-USSR, and a Canadian Forces CF-105D plane.

POINTE-AUX-TREMBLES WINDMILL

11630, rue Notre-Dame Est (corner of 3ᵉ avenue)
- Open to the public Saturday and Sunday, 12 noon to 5 pm, mid-June to early September
- Tel: 514 872 2240
- Bus lines 86 and 189 (Notre-Dame / 3ᵉ avenue stop)

Twenty names to remember

Who are the twenty people whose names are spelled out on the modern benches encircling the Pointe-aux-Trembles windmill?

The beautiful structure at 11630, rue Notre-Dame Est, a residential neighbourhood, is one of the last windmills in Quebec, which once had as many as 200. Today, only eighteen remain.

The first one, built in 1626, has disappeared without a trace, and the Pointe-aux-Trembles windmill nearly met the same fate in the 1960s–70s.

In 1719, the Sulpician priests who governed Montreal built this windmill at the north-eastern end of the island to replace one built previously in 1671–72, destroyed by a spring flood in 1718. Master builder Jean-Baptiste Deguire, also known as Larose, was contracted. Built traditionally in fieldstone, the windmill was used to make flour, although it also served as a fortress when the settlement was attacked. The mill ran at full capacity throughout most of the 18th century, but experienced a long period of inactivity in the 19th. In 1822, another floor was added to house a second millstone and thus increase the mill's productivity. This addition made it Quebec's tallest mill (at 13.7 metres), but not its widest (5.3 metres diameter), hence its beautifully slender appearance. The mill operated until 1861, and by the turn of the 20th century its sails were gone. It risked demolition on several occasions in the 20th century; a funeral home was even built right in front of it in the 1960s.

In 2001, thanks to the intervention of the Pointe-aux-Trembles historical society, the city acquired the historic building and the surrounding land. They demolished the funeral home in summer 2005 and began renovation work in 2007. The mill was straightened (subsidence was causing it to lean), new sails were added, and the interior beams were replaced, so that the mill once again looked as it did in the mid-20th century.

Since then, an interpretive trail with multimedia exhibits and informative "millstones" invites visitors to experience this historic and cultural site. A lookout point has also been built with a good view of the river.

The names engraved on the benches are those of the twenty millers who once operated the mill.

SANCTUAIRE DU SACRÉ-COEUR

3650, boulevard de La Rousselière (between 48ᵉ and 50ᵉ avenues)
• Tel: 514 642 5391
• Bus lines 40, 86 and 187 (De La Rousselière / Prince Arthur stop)

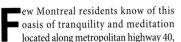

An urban oasis

Few Montreal residents know of this oasis of tranquility and meditation located along metropolitan highway 40, near 50ᵉ avenue in the Pointe-aux-Trembles district. Nevertheless, this place of worship must be very popular given the size of the parking lot, which was nearly empty the day of our visit. Except for the main religious holidays and days of pilgrimage, the sanctuary reposes in perfect peace.

The first point of interest is the Chapelle de la Réparation (Chapel of Atonement), rebuilt in 1910 on the ashes of the original late 19th-century monument. A large golden statue of Christ the Redeemer set atop the steeple seems to welcome visitors with open arms. A small welcome kiosk provides information about the history of the Sanctuary and its founder, Marie Hébert de La Rousselière. Born in Angers, France, in 1840, this devout Catholic devoted her life to the promotion of Eucharistic works. She first lived in Paris, where she founded the Association des Prêtres Adorateurs (Association of the Adoring Priests) devoted to the glory of Christ in the Eucharist. In 1886, she arrived in Montreal with the rich Brisset des Nos family, a son of which had married her sister Clémentine before deciding to flee the wave of anticlericalism that had taken over France. Upon arriving in Quebec, Marie continued her religious activities, with the goal of building a sanctuary dedicated to the work of the Atonement in Sacré-Coeur. Her brother-in-law had bought a large property surrounded by woods just a few miles away from Montreal, with the intention of spending the summer there. The beauty of the trees, its picturesque setting and the great solitude that pervaded the site made it perfect for prayer and meditation. La Rousselière had found the right place for her sanctuary.

In 1896, a wooden chapel was built, and a Way of the Cross was created in the adjacent woods the following year. Next came a replica of the Lourdes Grotto and a Scala Santa (in reference to the "Holy Stairs" in Rome) made of reinforced concrete and in a style reminiscent of a Byzantine church. After the death of her sister in December 1900, Marie Hébert de La Rousselière returned to France, where she later joined the Carmelite nuns in Angers. She died in 1924, at the age of 84. In the meantime, the Montreal sanctuary had become an important pilgrimage site. Led first by Dominican monks then by the Fathers of the Blessed Sacrament until 1918, the sanctuary was led by secular priests for a time before its current guardians, the Capuchin monks, arrived in 1921. The monks had a monastery built east of the Chapel of Atonement in 1922. Even more pilgrims came to visit the chapel after the Second World War. In 1946, an open chapel was built in the woods to mark the 50th anniversary of the creation of the sanctuary. Today the presence of this tranquil site in the middle of a growing residential neighbourhood, just a few kilometres from the refineries of north Montreal, is quite a surprise.

PARC DU BOUT DE L'ÎLE

Pointe-aux-Trembles
From rue Notre-Dame Est, turn right on terrasse Sainte-Maria Goretti
and take another right on 100ᵉ avenue to join rue Bureau, turn left to
find the park entrance about 100 metres ahead
• Bus line 86 (100ᵉ avenue stop)

A firm favourite

At the eastern end of Montreal Island, the Rivière des Prairies joins the Rivière des Milles Îles and the Saint Lawrence. At this symbolic site, there's a little park that apparently wasn't important enough to be named after a famous figure. It's simply called the Parc du Bout de l'Île (Island's End Park).

The park has a children's playground, a beautiful avenue of trees and, at the water's edge, a large boulder where you can sit and admire the landscape.

For a lover's tryst, a break during a bike ride, or a family picnic, this quiet park will become a firm favourite.

Opposite the park, you can see the town of Repentigny and a string of islands in the middle of the Saint Lawrence bearing rather evocative names. For example, the large island on the left, through which Route 138 – the famous Chemin du Roy, or King's Highway – runs on its way to Quebec, is called Île Bourdon (Bumblebee Island).

If you're looking for another nice place to stroll nearby, take rue Bureau, turn left on 94ᵉ avenue and follow it to terrasse Bellerive. This long, straight street is bordered by a cycle path and a grassy area along the riverbank. A few small motorboats are moored to the wooden jetties. Across the water, you'll see Île Sainte-Thérèse, part of which is a nature reserve. In the mid-1950s, rumour had it that a tunnel connecting Montreal to the South Shore would run through Île Sainte-Thérèse. Property values rose sharply and farmers sold their land, but in the end the tunnel was never built and the island fell back into its calm oblivion.

How many Montreal residents know that true happiness can be found here, just a stone's throw from the city centre?

NEARBY

PROMENADE BELLERIVE

8300, rue Bellerive. Take Notre-Dame Est towards the head of the island, turn right on rue Lebrun then right again onto rue Bellerive

In the 1960s, the banks of what is now Bellerive park were no more than 20 metres away from rue Bellerive. In the summer, people from the neighbourhood would go swimming, fishing or boating there. During the construction of the Louis-Hippolyte-Lafontaine Tunnel, from 1963 to 1967, thousands of tonnes of earth were dumped along promenade Bellerive, widening the banks by 240 metres over a distance of 2.2 kilometres. The infrastructure of the park only began to be added in 1997, thanks to the support of local residents. A reception lodge was built, thus marking the opening of Bellerive park. Since 1995, every summer a floating dock is installed near the west belvedere to accommodate a river shuttle service to the Boucherville Islands. A permanent stage was built in 2001 to host concerts and other events. The park offers several other activities: fishing lessons, bird watching, boat watching (Montreal's Old Port is very close), outdoor dancing events, and more. Discover the park in all its splendour during the Saint-Jean festivities in late June.

PARC NATIONAL DES ÎLES-DE-BOUCHERVILLE

55, Île Sainte-Marguerite
From Montreal, take Île Charron exit on highway 25 (after tunnel)
Tel: 450 928 5088

At the exit of the tunnel connecting Montreal to the south bank of the Saint Lawrence River, five islands and a few islets form the Îles-de-Boucherville National Park, right in the middle of the river. This national park offers 21 kilometres of cycle paths, 28 kilometres of hiking trails, canoe and kayak rental, numerous picnic areas, and countless activities led by experienced guides – everything you need to spend an excellent day. A small, rope-pulled boat connects Île Sainte-Marguerite to Île à Pinard, from May to October. On the islands, you can spot over 240 land and aquatic bird species and get so close to the white-tailed deer that you could almost pet them. They've found the territory of their dreams here on these islands.

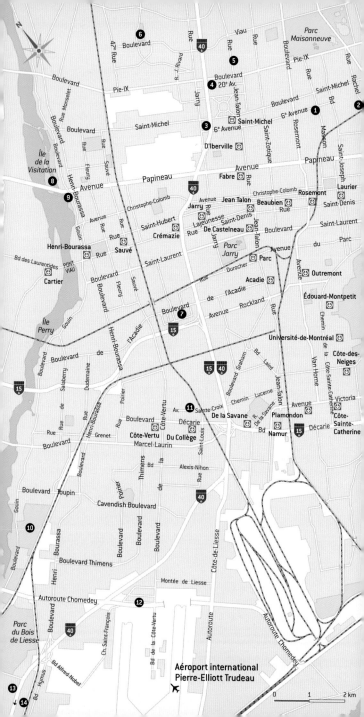

ROSEMONT, MONTREAL NORTH AND THE WEST OF THE ISLAND

ÉGLISE SAINT-ESPRIT-DE-ROSEMONT ❶

2851, rue Masson (between 5ᵉ and 6ᵉ avenues)
• Open every morning
• Mass held Monday to Friday at 8:30 am (Sunday at 9 am and 11 am)
• Métro: Laurier and bus 47 eastbound
• Tel: 514 376 3920

> **Montreal's only Art Deco church**

A t the heart of old Rosemont, Saint-Esprit is the only Art Deco church in Montreal, and one of the few in all of Canada.

In the 1920s, hundreds of families moved into this working-class neighbourhood, and the chapel soon became too small for the parish. Construction of a church began on this site in 1922, but the upper section wasn't started until 1931 and was finally completed in 1933. For ten years, the congregation had to worship in the basement.

As Art Deco was the popular movement of the 1930s, its modern style was the natural choice for Sainte-Philomène church (it became Saint-Esprit in 1964). The Great Depression, added to the fact that most of the city's churches had already been built at the time, is primarily why this is the city's only remaining Art Deco church.

The monument's typically clean and elegant lines include a flat ceiling whose decoration is an integral part of the structure, in the same way as the four angels attached to the exterior façade, or the Way of the Cross triptych sculpture that seems to emerge from the access ramp to the upper gallery. Nothing breaks the overriding sense of harmony. The only more lavish elements are the stained-glass windows by master artist Guido Nincheri, and the neo-Gothic steeple that was dismantled in 1949 when explosions at a nearby stone quarry destabilized it.

The magnificent Casavant organ (by a prominent North American organ builder) was damaged due to water infiltration, but a campaign to finance its restoration was launched in 2010.

Over the years, contrary to other churches in Montreal, the interior decor has remained intact, which is why Saint-Esprit church earned its spot on the city's list of heritage monuments in 1991.

FORMER ANGUS WORKSHOPS

2925, rue Rachel Est
• Open daily 8 am to 9 pm
• Métro: Préfontaine

A crane in a supermarket!

Until 1991, this tall red-brick building, now a supermarket, was an immense locomotive repair workshop. Inside, you can still see a huge yellow horizontal crane high above. Two such cranes were needed to lift a locomotive so that it could be inspected, tuned and repaired.

Named the Locoshop, the original building was 406 metres long. It was divided into two during demolition and all that is left today is the half occupied by the supermarket and a single brick wall hiding a car park. Supported by metal braces and lined by plants, this phantom wall that seems to rise out of nowhere simulates the continuation of the former workshop when seen from rue Rachel.

In the early 20th century, the Locoshop stood at the heart of the Shops Angus industrial complex, named after one of the directors and founders of the Canadian Pacific Railway Company.

Inaugurated in 1904, the Shops Angus complex was a city within a city. Covering over 5 square kilometres, it comprised sixty-eight buildings, the longest of which was over half a kilometre. At its period of peak production, some 12,000 workers were employed here. A workers' neighbourhood was built to house them; it became the Rosemont district in 1910.

The factory was self-sufficient: steel came in at one end and huge steam engines and carriages came out at the other.

During the two world wars, the factory's work was interrupted in order to manufacture shells (1914–1918) and, from 1939 to 1944, 1,700 Valentine tanks that were sent to Russia to reinforce the Red Army.

In the 1960s and 1970s, given the decline of the rail industry in favour of the automobile, the Angus factories suffered. Slowly but surely, the workshops were closed and the properties were evacuated. On January 31, 1992, the last locomotive repaired in the Angus Workshops passed through the factory doors.

Today, the company's activities continue in Winnipeg, Manitoba. In the late 1990s, the supermarket took over the Locoshop next to the former fire and police stations. The building, famous for its square tower with a high-point roof, is now home to a branch of the SAQ (Société des Alcools du Québec). That's all that's left of Shops Angus.

ÉGLISE SAINT-BERNARDIN-DE-SIENNE ❸

7979, 8ᵉ avenue, Saint-Michel
• Tel: 514 721 3411
• Métro: Saint-Michel
• Mass: Sunday at 9:30 am

A rocket and a hangar ...

How can you fail to notice Saint-Bernardin-de-Sienne church, located along the Metropolitan highway on 8ᵉ avenue, with its white, rocket-shaped steeple and its main building shaped like an aircraft hangar? When it was built in 1956, the innovative design of the church clashed with the Saint-Michel district which, before the Second World War, had still been composed of vast swathes of farms and allotments worked by farmers and market gardeners.

The Saint-Bernardin-de-Sienne parish was created in 1911 and the first Masses were held in a hall from a neighbouring parish. They had transported the whole thing by chaining it to logs pulled by horses.

What a contrast to the modern architecture of this church designed by architects Duplessis, Labelle and Derôme. Right away, visitors are struck by the building's size: the transept is 26 metres (86 ft) wide and 52 metres (172 ft) long.

Vast stained-glass windows let in light above the organ and at each end of the transept. Inside, the absence of beams adds to the great sense of space of this vessel decorated by lights that follow the roof's conical shape. The slits in the light fittings produce a play of light along the walls, and the numerous coloured-glass windows placed in staggered rows in the vault of the choir create beautiful effects. At night, when it is lit up from the inside, the church glows in a multitude of colours.

The wooden and Swedish blue granite furniture was also designed by the architects. The steeple, which isn't connected to the building, encloses a carillon of four bells manufactured in France. They were made by a foundry worker in Orleans and transported across the Atlantic by ship. Each of the bells, from the smallest (232 kg) to the largest (808 kg), was baptized on arrival by Quebec Cardinal Paul-Émile Léger: Saint Pie X, Joseph Alide, Paul-Émile and Eugène thus form a true carillon.

Unfortunately, Saint-Bernardin-de-Sienne is in danger. A victim of pollution and the vibrations of the nearby highway, it is in a critical condition and needs some costly repairs. Given the parish's dwindling congregation, the church may have to be sold in the coming years or, in the worst-case scenario, demolished.

PLACE DE L'UNITÉ

④

7655, 20ᵉ avenue, along boulevard Crémazie Est
• Tel: 514 722 2477
• Métro: Saint-Michel

*Remembering
Haiti*

Along the Metropolitan highway, at the intersection of 20ᵉ avenue and boulevard Crémazie, you'll find a very pretty fountain surrounded by statues in tribute to Haiti.

This small place de l'Unité (Unity Square), which commemorates the past of the first black republic in history, was created in May 2007, in front of the former Saint-Damasse church, which is now home to the "La Perle Retrouvée" Haitian Cultural Centre.

The four statues and two busts represent key figures of the Haitian Revolution, which led to the country's independence on January 1, 1804, and the end of the French colony of Saint-Domingue. Here, you'll find Toussaint Louverture, the hero of the 1791 Slave Revolt, Jean-Jacques Dessalines, or Jacques I, Haiti's first emperor, Alexandre Pétion, the first president of the republic of southern Haiti, and Henry Christophe, president then king of northern Haiti.

The two busts depict Sanite Bélaire, Toussaint Louverture's lieutenant, and Catherine Flon, who is believed to have created the Haitian flag. The story goes that in 1802, at the Congress of Arcahaie, after Jean-Jacques Dessalines tore off the white stripe representing the monarchy from the French flag, Catherine Flon sewed together the red and blue stripes using her hair for thread. The Haitian flag was born.

Since its creation, place de l'Unité has become a symbolic meeting place for Montreal's Haitian community. The Saint-Michel district, where it is located, is the Montreal neighbourhood with the largest number of Haitian residents. The "La Perle Retrouvée" association strives to promote Haitian culture through traditional dance, choral singing, Creole language courses, dinner shows and voodoo-inspired events. Haitians from the world over are invited to participate in funding the association's activities by buying bronze plaques which are then placed around the bases of the statues.

MINI-PUTT JEAN-TALON GOLF COURSE ❺

4400, rue Jean-Talon Est, Saint-Léonard
• Open all summer
• Métro: Saint-Michel

*Another
era!*

Who would believe that this ageing miniature golf course at the back of a shopping centre car park once had its hour of glory in the spotlight of an extremely popular television show? It all began in 1970 when Jean Benoît imported the concept of miniature golf, which was completely unknown in Quebec at the time. He created the Mini-Putt brand and franchise and, in three years, around 200 courses were built throughout the province. The first one was the Mini-Putt Jean-Talon. A fad was born. This new pastime, first designed as a fun family activity, quickly became a really competitive sport. Numerous tournaments were organized, attracting up to 1,000 participants. Elite players, amateurs, men, women and children faced one another in various categories. But, in 1989, with the arrival of TVSQ (Quebec Sports Television), now RDS (Sports Network), this new "sport" captivated the public. In the early 1990s, some 1.2 million viewers were glued to their TV screens to watch the weekly Mini-Putt Challenge show broadcast from the Jean-Talon course. It was an unprecedented smash hit for the channel, with audience ratings placing it just after the Montreal Expos baseball games!

The heroes of these televised games are the champions Carl Carmoni, the couple Suzanne and André Buis, Jocelyn Noël "the eternal runner-up", Gilles "The Champ" Bussières, and let's not forget commentator Serge Vleminx and his famous "Biiiiiiiiirdie!" scream. Unfortunately, the Mini-Putt was a victim of its own success. In the mid-1990s, there were so many courses in some towns that they practically touched one another. New franchises arrived and the competition became quite fierce. Then came the bad years. Hundreds

of courses closed and, in the late 1990s, the televised games had trouble finding enough commercial sponsors to finance the show. The 2000 season was the last for the Mini-Putt Challenge, which went off the air definitively. Carl Carmoni, who still organizes a dozen or so tournaments a year in Quebec, hopes to revive the sport of miniature golf, and even bring it back to television. That would be the perfect opportunity to rejuvenate the Jean-Talon course.

SAINT LEONARD CAVE

Parc Pie-XII
5200, boulevard Lavoisier
• Tel: 514 252 3323
• Open late May to mid-August
• Tours Tuesday to Saturday, reservations required at least two weeks prior to visit • $10 (adults) and $9 (discount) • Minimum age: 6
• Bus 132 (Viau stop) and 32 (Cadillac stop), northbound

Urban caving

I f while in Pie XII park you come across a group of a dozen people equipped with rubber boots and gloves, and wearing a hard hat and headlamp, you're not hallucinating. It's simply a group of visitors of Saint Leonard cave, a site of speleological exploration, rarely found within the city limits.

The temperature of this cave, which reaches a depth of 9 metres, never tops 5 °C (41 °F), and the humidity is almost 100%. Add the mud covering the cave floor and it's not hard to see why visitors have to wear so much gear.

Numerous stories and legends have been told about this site (American Indians supposedly lived here before the Europeans arrived; the Patriots of the 1837 rebellion against the occupying English forces are said to have used it as a weapons stockpile), but none of these speculations have been proven by the scientific studies conducted here.

The general public didn't discover the existence of this cave until an article about it was published in *Le Spectateur* newspaper in 1835. In the 1960s, it was the playground for the pupils of the nearby Pie XII school. The children knew exactly where the hole in the ground that led to the cave was. In 1979, the site was finally recognized by the city, which decided to officially open it to the public in 1981. The cave, also called the "Fairy Hole", was thus adapted to welcome visitors.

Now steps lead down into the cave and an entrance door keeps out intruders. The tours are organized by the Société Québécoise de Spéléologie (Quebec Caving Society). Every descent into the cave is led by an experienced guide who introduces you to the mysteries of the formation of these passages created millions of years ago by the movement of glaciers. After a short slideshow about the world of caving, the visitors begin their exploration in a long passage roughly 13 metres long, 3 metres wide and 2 metres high. Here, they can observe the different strata of the soil, several fossils, and, in a small niche, stalactites and stalagmites that unfortunately have been broken by vandals. Then, the passage narrows and arrives at a junction where ladders lead down a shaft to the main vein, 5 metres below. The entire path covers some 35 metres. The tours, which last 1 hour and 45 minutes, are only offered in summer – the perfect opportunity to escape the heat. Every year, more than 3,000 lucky visitors discover this unique site.

LUFA GREENHOUSES

❼

1400, rue Antonio-Barbeau
• Tel: 514 669 3559 • https://lufa.com
• Bus lines 179 and 365 (de L'Acadie / Legendre stop)
• Tours organized during Open House days held every three months

Urban agriculture on a rooftop

Opened in 2011, the Lufa farm is the first commercial greenhouse in the world installed on a rooftop.

Located at 1400, rue Antonio-Barbeau near the Marché Central shopping centre, south of boulevard de l'Acadie, it is perched on a building at the heart of a block of commercial warehouses – a rather unexpected place for an organic greenhouse.

Yet it looks sharp with its large plate-glass windows and aluminium and galvanized steel frame. At first, the challenge was daunting: to use responsible agriculture techniques to grow organic vegetables year round on a rooftop measuring almost 3,000 square metres (31,000 feet), which is twice the size of Centre Bell arena's ice rink.

Some twenty-five types of vegetables and herbs are grown here without the use of pesticides, fungicides or herbicides. Everything is done organically. For example, insects are deliberately introduced to help control other harmful pests.

On the tours organized during the Open House days, visitors must wear a white coat, wash their hands and walk through a footbath in order to preserve the greenhouse's natural balance.

The results of this agricultural method are flavourful, quality vegetables. To keep all their freshness, the products are delivered within a radius of 5 kilometres around the urban farm. If you want to taste them, you'll have to sign up for a weekly "basket" containing a selection of lettuces, tomatoes, cucumbers, peppers, aubergines, Chinese cabbage, fresh herbs, and more. The selection is crated then distributed at a convenient pick-up spot near you.

According to experts, such greenhouses could be installed on 10% of Canada's urban rooftops.

SAULT-AU-RÉCOLLET WINDMILLS

Parc de l'Île-de-la-Visitation – 2425, boulevard Gouin Est
- Tel: 514 280 6733
- Maison du Meunier museum and bistro – 10897, rue du Pont
- Tel: 514 850 4222 and 514 850 0322
- Métro: Henri-Bourassa
- Bus 69 Gouin Est, rue Saint-Firmin or rue Parthenais stops

> *"I can't believe we're in Montreal!"*

"I can't believe we're in Montreal!", visitors exclaim when they arrive at Île-de-la-Visitation Nature Park for the first time. Both nature reserve and historic site, this park established in 1984 is in the north-west of the island, in the extension of avenue Papineau along the Rivière des Prairies.

Few Montreal residents know of this 34 hectare site and the footpath that leads through its magnificent wooded shores and to the numerous remains of an agricultural and industrial past that dates back to the early 18th century.

In 1724, miller Simon Sicard began the construction of a dyke over 100 metres long connecting the island of Montreal to the small Île de la Visitation (called Branchereau at the time) on property owned by the Sulpician monks. The first mills fed by the river's rapids were installed to cut timber, and then to make flour. The Maison du Meunier (Miller's House) was built in 1727. It still stands today and is home to a charming bistro and a small museum about the general stores of the early 1900s. The dozen or so tables on the terrace overlook a pretty waterfall that adds to the site's bucolic charm and makes it the perfect place to begin a romantic summer evening.

With the invention of the turbine in the 1830s, the windmill site took an industrial turn. Flour was still manufactured here, but so was cardboard made from old newspapers, rags and recuperated leather. The mills became one of the region's biggest employers and continued to function until the late 1970s.

Bought by the city, the site was left abandoned for about twenty years before the authorities decided to turn it into a heritage site. The brick factory walls were demolished so that only the old fieldstone walls remained. Trees were planted among the ruins to symbolize the space once occupied by the mills. The entirety of the new site, which opened in 1998, was placed in the hands of the Cité Historia association, which is responsible for its management and development. From spring to autumn, guides in period costume offer tours, some of which are aboard a little train, a replica of a 1920s tram.

STATUE OF AHUNTSIC

9

Église de la Visitation grounds – 1847, boulevard Gouin Est
• Métro: Henri-Bourassa

*Mystery
surrounding
a historic figure*

The character named Ahuntsic, whose statue embellishes the grounds of the Church of the Visitation not far from the statue of Father Nicolas Viel, remains shrouded in mystery.

The statue carved in stone depicts Ahuntsic as an American Indian. The plaque at the foot of the statue reads: "*This monument was erected on 24 May 1903 by the parishioners of Sault-au-Récollet to perpetuate the memory of the heroic death of the young novice Ahuntsic, precipitated by evil Hurons, along with his spiritual father Nicolas Viel, a Recollect, at the last rapids of the Rivière des Prairies in spring 1625.*" This is the account that Jesuit missionary Paul Le Jeune gave in 1636 about the death of what he called the "first two Canadian martyrs". Another account is engraved on a granite stele in the nearby Nicolas Viel Park: "*Into these rapids the Recollect Father Nicolas Viel and his novice the Huron Ahuntsic, the first Canadian martyrs, were thrown by their pagan guides in hatred of the faith on 25 June 1625. This place has since been known as Sault-au-Récollet.*" This first version of the death of these two historic figures was undermined by the account of Swedish naturalist Peter Kalm who visited the site in 1749: "*He (Nicolas Viel) was canoeing down the river with a converted savage and several other savages of the Huron nation on their way to Quebec. But as they passed this section of the river, the canoe capsized and he drowned, along with his novice.*" This novice was Ahuntsic, who was described as an "educated and baptized" Huron; so he apparently wasn't assassinated, but rather drowned by accident. In 1942, the brave Ahuntsic lost his status as an American Indian when Franciscan Archange Godbout demonstrated that he was actually a young Frenchman, and not a Huron. Ahuntsic, or "Auhaïtsique", was the nickname the Hurons gave to this young adventurer, naming him after a small, quick and rapid fish.

In recent years, as the murder theory has been disproven, the authorities have decided to modify the symbols referring to this mysterious episode of Montreal's past. The 1926 plaque on the façade of the church was changed and now reads: "*Here, at the last rapids of Rivière des Prairies, on 25 June 1625, Recollect Nicolas Viel and his young compatriot nicknamed Auhaïtsic drowned.*" The stele at Nicolas Viel park has also been changed. In October, 2010, the inscription was covered with a black marble plaque that reads: "*On June 25, 1625, Nicolas Viel and his fellow countryman, nicknamed Auhaïtsic by the Huron-Wendats, perished in these rapids. This place has since been known as Sault-au-Récollet.*"

Quebec historian Jean-Pierre Sawaya, fascinated by colonist-American Indian relations, is not surprised by these various interpretations. "The history of French-Indian relations is old and not everything was recorded. There's a lot of hearsay, and that's part of our heritage. Even if there's no certitude, that's OK, because it feeds our imagination. That's what the history of Quebec is made of."

BOIS-DE-SARAGUAY

9095, boulevard Gouin Ouest
• Park entrance on avenue Jean-Bourdon
• Bus lines 68, 382, 468 (Gouin /Joseph-Saucier stop)

A primal forest

Unfairly overlooked, the Bois-de-Saraguay Nature Park is the most beautiful and oldest forest of Montreal island. It is also the best preserved. The woods are home to over 350 plant species and several centuries-old trees. Besides the silver maple, white elm, red ash and black ash, you'll find rare varieties, such as the black maple, swamp white oak and common hackberry.

137 species of bird have been recorded here, as well as several mammals, including beaver, muskrat and marmot. In the early 18th century, the first observers of the vegetation on Montreal island noted the quality of the Saraguay woods and commonly called it the "Good Wood". The park almost disappeared in 1979 to make way for a high-rise apartment building project. Thanks to lobbying by several associations, it was saved and declared a natural district in 1981, then a nature park, even though it has never really been developed or officially opened to the public. This treasure of biodiversity is protected behind its gates and is still listed as a "park-to-be", although walking trails already cover the 97 hectares of this marshland area and its gates are open all year round.

NEARBY

MACDOUGALL MANOR

9095, boulevard Gouin Ouest
Corner avenue Jean-Bourdon and avenue Joseph-Saucier

In addition to its woods, Bois-de-Saraguay also comprises the Ogilvy property, Île aux Chats, and the Mary Dorothy Molson House, also called MacDougall Manor. The estate recalls the luxurious era of the well-to-do English-speaking families who, in the early 20th century, moved into the extravagant homes of the village of Saraguay, along the Rivière des Prairies. Today, MacDougall Manor remains one of the neighbourhood's most well-preserved homes. Built in 1930 by architect Alexander Tilloch Galt Durnford, it was owned by the Molson-MacDougall family until the 1970s. The Montreal Urban Community acquired it in 1981. Today, it is one of the historic monuments protected by the City of Montreal. Since 1998, the manor has served as a location for film and television productions, but plans to open it to the public are under consideration.

MUSÉE DES MAÎTRES ET ARTISANS DU QUÉBEC

⓫

615, avenue Sainte-Croix (Saint-Laurent district)
• Tel: 514 747 7367
• Métro: Du-Collège
• Open Wednesday to Sunday, 12 noon to 5 pm
• Admission: $7 adults, $4 students

A rich and original collection in prestigious surroundings

A rich and original collection in prestigious surroundings: a phrase that perfectly sums up Quebec's Masters and Artisans Museum, located on the CEGEP Saint-Laurent campus, avenue Sainte-Croix.

Indeed, the museum occupies the magnificent neo-Gothic Saint Paul's Presbyterian church that once graced boulevard Dorchester (now René-Lévesque Ouest). In 1931, the church was expropriated to make way for a train station. The Fathers of Sainte-Croix bought it for one symbolic dollar. In two months, the church was dismantled and rebuilt stone by stone on the property of the CEGEP Saint-Laurent (a general and vocational school), and was used as the school's Catholic chapel. When the school system was secularized, the church became the home of the Saint-Laurent Art Museum, founded in 1979. It was converted into the Museum of Masters and Artisans in 2003; the church was renovated for the occasion.

The museum's impressive collection of more than 10,000 objects relating to the arts and artisan traditions of Quebec from the 17th century to the present day clearly strives to transmit this knowledge through the generations. Some 400 objects compose the new permanent exhibition, "From Master's Hands". An audio guide recorded by storyteller Fred Pellerin leads you through the exhibit, where you can discover furniture, fabrics, various personal and religious objects, toys, jewellery, and statues that marked the everyday lives of French Canadians over the centuries. The central section of the former church, with its magnificent carved wooden vaults, is given over to temporary exhibits.

THE "PLANESPOTTERS" OF BOULEVARD PITFIELD

Along highway 13 at intersection with boulevard de la Côte-Vertu
• Bus line 174 (Côte-Vertu / Pitfield stop)

> *Montreal, a "planespotter's" paradise*

They are called "planespotters" or "plane-spotting" enthusiasts. Every day, this original activity attracts several thousand people to aviation fields all around the world. Their hobby: watching planes as they take off or land, taking photos, checking flight times, and even noting the aircraft registration numbers so they can look up technical details of the examples they've observed.

Montreal is one of the best places in the world for planespotters. Indeed, most airports are very strict and refuse access to those who get too close to the fences around the landing strips, but this isn't the case at Pierre Elliot Trudeau International, where relations with the airport authorities remain friendly. In return, it is not unknown for the planespotters to inform airport security of potential dangers.

Numerous "spots" all around the two large strips thus attract planespotters. The best known is located in the cul-de-sac of boulevard Pitfield, near highway 13, right at the end of the large strip where the largest planes generally land. The best time to come is in the early afternoon when the first international flights arrive: the planes pass right over the heads of observers (it'll blow you away!), and the engine noise in landing position isn't too loud.

But now, boulevard Pitfield has some stiff competition. In May 2012, Montreal airport opened Jacques-de-Lesseps park, named after the French aviation pioneer who was the first to fly over Montreal in 1910. The park, at the corner of rue Halpern and rue Jenkins, was especially designed for planespotters: several benches and a small platform allow around thirty people to observe the planes close up.

THIR MURUGAN TEMPLE

1611, boulevard Saint-Regis, Dollard-Des-Ormeaux
- Tel: 514 683 8044
- Open 8 am to 1:30 pm and 5 pm to 9 pm
- Pooja (ceremony) at 9 am, noon and 5 pm
- Métro: Côte-Vertu then bus 215 to 1611, Saint Regis stop

Another world on the street corner

They say Montreal is the city of a hundred steeples, but it is also a city of mosques, synagogues and oriental temples.

The Thiru Murugan temple, at 1611, boulevard Saint-Regis in Dollard-Des-Ormeaux, is one of the most beautiful. It stands out in this residential district far from the tourist circuit.

The site deserves a visit. Designed by nine Indian architects, the Thiru Murugan temple was the first in Canada to be built according to the age-old rites of Shaivism, a branch of the Hindu religion primarily followed in southern India and Sri Lanka.

Montreal's Tamil community, made up of roughly 20,000 residents, inaugurated the temple in 2006. It reproduces an original Indian architecture to near perfection.

Very impressive on the outside with its tower and finely sculpted white cornices, the temple has a surprisingly large interior hall dotted with numerous small altars to various divinities. It abounds with colour and exotic fragrances, which transport you to the other side of the world.

The guardians of this site are glad to welcome people of other faiths. They simply ask that you be discreet and respectful, and that you remove your shoes at the entrance.

ANOTHER TEMPLE IN THE WEST OF THE ISLAND

NANAK DARBAR SIKH TEMPLE

7801, rue Cordner in LaSalle
- Tel: 514 595 1881
- Métro: Angrignon and bus 109, boulevard Shevchencko southbound, Cordner-Chopin stop

Built in 2001 by the Sikh community, the Nanak Darbar Sikh temple is a veritable palace out of the *Arabian Nights*. This large white building with golden domes soars to over 21 metres and is one of the biggest Sikh temples in the world. Visitors are asked to remove their shoes and cover their hair (scarves are provided).

CHEMIN DE SENNEVILLE

• Bus line 68 (Gouin / Lauzon stop)

*Heritage
hidden ...
by trees*

Chemin de Senneville is a small road connecting Sainte-Anne-de-Bellevue and Senneville along Lac des Deux-Montagnes (Lake of Two Mountains). Roughly 7 kilometres long, it begins at rue Sainte-Anne north of highway 20, passes through the village of Senneville north of highway 40, and then heads north-west to join up with boulevard Gouin at the intersection with chemin de l'Anse-à-l'Orme. A trip through this west side of Montreal island is a real foray into the country, as this is where you'll find the remaining farms, wooded areas, meadows, orchards and vast shoreline properties hidden behind long stone walls.

Senneville is among the oldest settlements in Quebec. In 1679, Michel-Sidrac Dugué, an officer of the French army and governor of Montreal Island, sold his Boisbriand fief to Jacques Le Ber and his fur-trading associate and brother-in-law, Charles LeMoyne. Jacques Le Ber renamed the Boisbriand fief Senneville, after his hometown in France (today, Senneville is a hamlet of Amfreville-sous-les-Monts in Normandy). A windmill and then a small fort were built on the fief, but they were later destroyed by fire. A number of colonists settled on this fertile ground, but it wasn't until 1895 that a group of citizens decided to found the village that still exists today. In the second half of the 19th century, Senneville became the privileged vacation destination for the Montreal well-to-do. At the time, the Grand Trunk Railway, inaugurated in 1865, provided fast and comfortable access to this still natural part of the island. The Dow, Abbott, Todd, Angus, Meredith, Morgan and Forget families, pillars of the Canadian economy, enjoyed the high life as they ranged between their city centre homes and large shoreline properties. They called on the best architects and landscapers of the period to construct and design their luxurious mansions. To highlight this synergy between Montreal's great financiers and some of the best Canadian builders of the time, the historic district of Senneville was declared a National Historic Site in 2002. In addition to the homes and their outbuildings (tea houses, employee residences, stables, cowsheds, garages, etc.), the site also comprises several nature areas , the most important of which are the Anse-à-l'Orme Nature Park, Bois-de-la-Roche Agricultural Park, Morgan Arboretum and Braeside Golf Course.

In most large cities, such rural vacation destinations were eventually engulfed by urban expansion and the construction of service and commercial buildings. This isn't the case at Senneville, where you still have the feeling of being in the middle of the country. Unfortunately, most of the historic sites of chemin de Senneville, including the ruins of the fort, are located on private property so are inaccessible. But you can still glimpse them from the lake, either by boat or, for the more adventurous, by a walk on the ice in winter.

ANSE-À-L'ORME NATURE PARK: WINDSURFER'S PARADISE

This 196 hectare park at the intersection of boulevard Gouin Ouest, chemin de Senneville and chemin de l'Anse-à-l'Orme is located along the shores of Lake of Two Mountains. Windsurfers and small sailboats converge here to enjoy the site's dominant west winds. A picnic area, outdoor showers and two boat launch ramps are available for public use.

BOIS-DE-LA-ROCHE AGRICULTURAL PARK

This vast country estate of 190 hectares plunges visitors into the ambiance of old-style farming. Notable features are buildings dating from the beginning of the 20th century, some of which are the work of the Maxwell brothers, renowned architects of their day. You can still see some of these in various states of repair by following the chemin de l'Anse-à-l'Orme.

The farm, set up in 1880 by the financier Louis-Joseph Forget, was run by his descendants until 1991. The estate was then taken over by the City of Montreal in order to preserve it. Since then, Bois-de-la-Roche has been on the list of the city's "parks-to-be".

ALPHABETICAL INDEX

ALPHABETICAL INDEX